Let's Eat Grandma?

A Workbook for Learning the Marvels of Punctuation and Improving your Writing Skills

Leonard Beeghley, Ph.D.

Cover and book design by Claudia Fulshaw Design, located in Durham, NC.

Published by Beginning Writers Press
Printed and distributed by Create Space

ISBN-13: 978-1724254559
ISBN-10: 1724254553

Dedication

To our beloved Greg, who adored his family,

enjoyed sports, and laughed at Captain Underpants

Table of Contents

Introduction 7

I. Let's Eat Grandma? 11

II. Period 13

III. Question Mark 16

IV. Exclamation Point 17

V. Rhetorical Fragments 18

VI. Comma 20

   1. Introducer Comma 21

     a. Worksheet #1 – Fred's Story 24

     b. Suggested Answers to Worksheet #1 25

     c. Worksheet #2 – Jonas's Story 28

     d. Suggested Answers to Worksheet #2 30

   2. Joiner Comma 33

     a. Worksheet #3 – Alligator Stew 37

     b. Suggested Answers to Worksheet #3 38

     c. Worksheet #4 – Matteo's Story 40

     d. Suggested Answers to Worksheet #4 42

   3. Inserter Commas 45

     a. Worksheet #5 – Escargots 47

     b. Suggested Answers to Worksheet #5 48

     c. Worksheet #6 – Anansi's Story 50

     d. Suggested Answers to Worksheet #6 51

   4. Linker Comma 53

     a. Worksheet #7 – Mindset 56

     b. Suggested Answers to Worksheet #7 57

     c. Worksheet #8 – Andrew's Suggestion 59

     d. Suggested Answers to Worksheet #8 60

   5. Looking Beyond the Comma to More Marvels of Punctuation 62

VII. Colon 63

1. Forward-looking colon 63

2. Spacer colon 65

3. Spacer Period and Comma 67

   a. Worksheet #9 – The Dentist...69

   b. Suggested Answers to Worksheet #9 70

VIII. Semicolon 73

1. Connector Semicolon 74

2. Managing Semicolon 76

IX. Using Punctuation Tools to Improve your Writing Skills 77

X. Back to the Future 82

1. Worksheet #10 – George and Harold's Revenge 84

2. Suggested Answers to Worksheet #10 86

XI. Improving Your Writing Skills and Changing the World 89

About the Author 91

Acknowledgments 92

Contact Me 93

Introduction

Most people don't think much about punctuation or its connection to writing well. You may even imagine that these little marks are unnecessary. After all, they did not exist for most of human history.[1]

maybe we should eliminate all those pesky marks the ancient Greeks got along wellwithoutthemtheydidnotevenincludespacesbetweenwordsi think the comma is stupid who cares about it all those other symbols are also needless especially the semicolon it is unnecessary you can always use a period instead or even an exclamation point but it is just an exploding period in sum it would be better to get rid of the whole system of punctuation if it was good enough for the Greeks then it is good enough for us readers will not mind

But readers do mind. And they are your audience. It does not matter whether you are writing a note to your Grandma, a school assignment for your teacher, or a memo to your boss. These little dots and squiggles provide some of the most important tools by which you express yourself to others.

The subtitle of this workbook refers to the "marvels of punctuation." The word marvel refers to something that is astounding or awe-inspiring. For example, in the Marvel Comics, superheroes use their special powers to perform amazing deeds. They fight against evil and save the innocent, at least in imagination.

Punctuation tools will not give you superpowers. But their impact is just as amazing. Your choice of punctuation tools influences what you say, how you say it, and what you mean. And, best of all, these effects occur in the real world, not an imaginary one.

In the real world, it is impossible to talk face-to-face all the time. You will sometimes have to put your thoughts in writing. As you learn to use punctuation tools effectively, your writing skills, your ability to communicate with readers, will improve as well. You might want to persuade them to purchase a copy of *Captain Underpants and the Attack of the Talking Toilets*, teach them how to draw like Dav Pilkey, or announce the first meeting of the Captain Underpants Fan Club.[2] Mr. Pilkey's writings are deliciously demented. Introducing your readers to his works probably won't change the world, but it might become a happier place. That's a start.

---

[1] On the history of punctuation, see David Crystal, *Making A Point: The Persnickety Story of English Punctuation* (New York: St. Martin's Press, 2015). Mr. Crystal opens his charming book with similar examples. The ancient Greeks did not use lower case letters. They were invented some time later.

[2] Dav Pilkey, *Captain Underpants and the Attack of the Talking Toilets.* (New York: Scholastic, 1999). Yes, Mr. Pilkey spells his first name without an "e" on the end but pronounces it "Dave."

This workbook provides the beginning writer with a toolbox of marks and the insight necessary to compose effective sentences and paragraphs. Modern English includes many punctuation tools by which writers can make their meaning clear. If you are just learning the craft, however, you can get along successfully by mastering just a few: the period, question mark, exclamation point, comma, colon, and semicolon. You will not be alone. Successful authors rely mainly on these six tools to write in a way that is easy to read and understand.

Although this guide is aimed at adolescents and young adults, any beginning writer can benefit from it. Mastering the marvels of punctuation improves your writing skills for a reason: You learn to consider your choices and think about what you want to say. Of course, these tools do not stand alone. Authors who write well also use simple words and compose relatively short sentences. Their paragraphs are brief as well. Their goal is to write plainly so that reading becomes a pleasure. You can achieve this goal, too.

As a teaching manual, this workbook displays some differences from others you may have read. Key words are defined to avoid confusion. Boldface and italics function to emphasize key points. The idea is to help you learn to write clearly, concisely, and with feeling, so that you influence readers.

This book arose from my experience helping immigrant and first generation Hispanic adolescents improve their writing skills. These young people are bright, articulate, and write expressively. But not always effectively. Like all beginning writers, they find it hard to use punctuation tools to control the rhythm and meaning of their sentences and paragraphs. As a result, they often do not communicate well when forced to use a pen or keyboard.

As an author myself, I have used these tools for decades. But knowing how to use them and explaining their use to others entail different skills. I needed teaching materials. Alas, that became a problem.

In matters of punctuation and writing, many teachers still rely on William Strunk and E.B. White's *Elements of Style*.[3] A century after its original publication in 1919, it remains an admired guide. It has sold millions of copies over the years and, in 2011, *Time* magazine named it one of the top 100 most influential nonfiction books of the last century.[4] But here are some secrets that few admit: The authors' writing style is painfully boring, their advice is rigidly rule-based, and their meaning often resembles a foggy swamp. Thus, while *Elements of Style* resides on many shelves, including mine, few have read it entirely. Including me.

Elements of Style is not unique in being hard to read and absorb. With a few exceptions, most guides to punctuation are not useful for teaching beginners to write well because they share the following problems:

---

[3] William Strunk and E. B. White, *Elements of Style* (New York: Macmillan, 1979).

[4] See *Time*, August 11, 2011. Better yet, look for "All-TIME 100 Nonfiction Books" with your search engine.

Let's Eat Grandma? © 2018 Leonard Beeghley

- Most guides to punctuation are mind-numbing to read. Even adults, for whom most books are written, find them tedious. And when worksheets are included they consist of random sentences that are not relevant to people's lives. Your time is valuable, why spend it being bored?

 By contrast, this workbook tells stories and uses humor to hold your attention while you learn. Because you are engaged with the text and worksheets, it becomes easier to remember the marvels of punctuation and think about improving your writing skills.

- Most guides introduce and explain punctuation marks in a disorganized way. In fact, the presentation appears random in most cases. Readers are given rules and examples, one following the other without any organizing principle. Without guidance, readers find it hard to become involved in the material.

 By contrast, this workbook is organized in two ways, as shown in the Table of Contents. The first is frequency. Marks that end sentences are considered in order of use: the period, question mark, and then the exclamation point. Similarly, marks within sentences are discussed in terms of how often they occur: the comma, the colon, and then the semicolon. The second organizing principle is to give marks names according to their function. Commas aren't just commas, they serve four different purposes. Each gets a name. Similarly, the names given to colons and semicolons reflect the different problems they solve. These two strategies make it easier for you to read, understand, and remember how to use punctuation tools effectively.

- Most guides are rule-based. Emphasizing rules leads to an unfortunate orientation by students. You learn to ask a question like this: What punctuation mark goes here? As if there was one right answer. But in punctuation, as in life, you always have choices. Your task is to pick wisely.

 By contrast, this workbook teaches you a tool-based approach to punctuation. You learn to ask a different question: How can I use punctuation tools to make my meaning clear and my writing provocative? Effective sentence structure and continuity do not depend on following rules; they reflect the judgment of a writer. Your judgment. Which you will learn in this book.

- Most guides focus on punctuating sentences. Sounds reasonable, right? But it is not. What do you do when a period, comma, colon, and semicolon are all grammatically correct choices? This problem occurs often. You cannot pick wisely by looking at a sentence in isolation.

 By contrast, this workbook emphasizes that sentences occur in paragraphs. Each paragraph tells a story or has a point to make. You choose the most effective punctuation tool in that context.

The need to choose among several marks implies a truth that should be self-evident but is often ignored: Improving your writing skills is hard work. Few sentences or paragraphs come out right the first time, certainly not mine. As William Zinsser points out, the essence of good writing is rewriting.[5] But the reward for all this effort is great. You inform, entertain, and influence others, sometimes people you don't even know. They might read *Captain Underpants and the Attack of the Talking Toilets.* That's an amazing deed, especially since a few misguided people would like to prevent you and others from enjoying this experience. The last worksheet deals with this book.[6]

This workbook is designed to be read, used, and abused. The lessons build upon each other. I recommend that you begin at the beginning, consider the examples, and go through each worksheet thoughtfully. About the worksheets: Students hate them. For this reason, I thought about using a different label for them, like "Eat a Cookie While You Test Yourself." But, really, they are what they are. Instead, enjoy the stories as you think about the punctuation and writing problems they pose. While you are doing that, use and abuse this book. Mark it up with a pen or highlighter. Write in the margins. Suggest alternatives to my answers. Build your skills. Learn judgment. The world awaits your insights.

Your Notes Here

_____

_____

_____

_____

_____

_____

_____

---

[5] See William Zinsser, *On Writing Well* (New York: Harper Collins, 2001), pp. x-xi. This is my favorite book on writing. It is also a good read. I bought an earlier edition in the late 1980s and read it cover-to-cover over two days. Reading this book helped me improve my writing and will help you, too.

[6] There are fourteen books in the Captain Underpants series. In 2012 and 2013, the series achieved an important honor. They were the books a few strait-laced people most often tried to ban from libraries and schools around the country. This is according the American Library Association, which publishes the results each year. Their site is: http://www.ala.org/advocacy/bbooks/frequentlychallengedbooks/top10, accessed March 6, 2018. Why do you think it is an honor when people attempt to ban a book or series from libraries and schools? Although the Captain Underpants books will not help you improve your writing, they will make you laugh. They might also make you think.

I.
Let's Eat Grandma?

No, she didn't really mean it. She didn't want to eat her grandma. After ten-year-old Melanie wrote *Let's eat Grandma.* and read it out loud, she looked up in horror. "I don't want to eat my abuela!" Fortunately, it was a misunderstanding, easily corrected by adding a simple mark. *Let's **eat,** Grandma.* When Melanie wrote this version and again read it aloud, she relaxed. Inserting the comma changed the meaning! The sentence now expressed her true intent: to share a meal with her beloved abuela.

Perhaps it would be a lunch of pupusas and orange juice. Pupusas, a food from El Salvador, consist of little cakes made of corn flour, filled with cheese or meat, and topped with salsa. One of the marvels of American life is that we take new foods, enjoy their unique flavors, and make them our own. This process enriches our diets, adds words to our language, and improves our lives.

Punctuation, those little dots, lines, and curlicues scattered within and between sentences, can improve your life as well. Thus, when you send a note asking your Grandma to lunch, she won't run away in fear. Instead, she'll see the comma and reply "what time?" This is your first lesson in the marvels of punctuation. There will be more.

Punctuation comprises a system of tools that serves three purposes in writing. Each affects your ability to express yourself clearly to others. **First, they end sentences, separating them from one another.** Periods (.), question marks (?), and exclamation points (!) tell you to stop before going on. **Second, they regulate the pace of a sentence.** Commas (,), colons (:), and semi-colons (;) tell you to pause and then go. Although other punctuation marks exist, these six provide beginners with the tools necessary to write logical sentences and paragraphs. **Third, they help make your meaning clear.** Surprisingly, as Melanie and her abuela know, whether you ask readers stop or pause before continuing effects their understanding of what you have written.

In this book, you will learn tool-based punctuation. A tool is a device with a specific purpose. The trick, of course, is to pick the correct tool for the job. A knife and fork are devices to help you eat. A hammer and nails are devices to help you build something. And punctuation marks are devices to help you write well. In writing, as in life, **tools are more effective than rules.** By **tool-based punctuation**, I mean the use of punctuation marks to control the rhythm and meaning of sentences and paragraphs.[7]

---

[7] Stephen King argues that beginning writers should develop a toolbox of skills. See his *On Writing: A Memoir of the Craft* (New York: Scribner, 2000). Roy Peter Clark points out that good writers use tools rather than obey rules, a line I shall use a lot. See his *Writing Tools: 55 Essential Strategies for Every Writer* (New York: Little Brown, 2006). Both of these books are good reads and will help you develop your talent.

When you establish a good tempo, sentences go faster or slower, as you intend. **The easiest thing for readers to do is quit**, which they will do if you bore them or confuse them. But when you fit everything together so that reading becomes a positive experience, they continue. The marvels of punctuation give you a kind of superpower: the ability to affect others' behavior. Because of you, readers want to be taught, persuaded, or entertained. In order to understand how punctuation tools help with these tasks, consider the difference between speaking and writing.

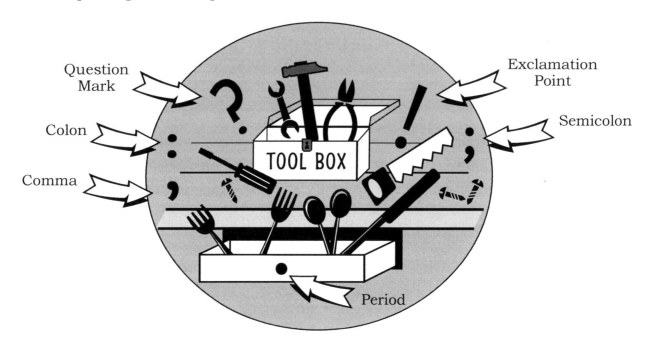

When speaking, you employ verbal and nonverbal signals in addition to the words. Sometimes, a verbal message changes the meaning of what you say. For example, laughing when you claim to have studied for a test suggests that perhaps you didn't. Volume, tone, hesitation, and stress can all influence meaning. Similarly, a physical gesture may change the meaning of your words, too. For example, rolling your eyes while claiming to have studied also implies you did not. People use hand movements, shoulder shrugs, frowns, and other physical gestures to communicate with each other. All these verbal and physical signals require face-to-face contact and none of them are available when we write. Punctuation tools solve this problem.

In solving it, punctuation tools empower you. These marks function like the hammer and nails used to build a house. You use them to hold your sentences and paragraphs together, allowing people to read and understand what you write. Just as hammering nails in the wrong place or forgetting to use them at all can lead to catastrophe, so it is with punctuation. Using these symbols without care can change the meaning of a sentence. Misunderstanding results.

You avoid misunderstanding by using simple and forceful language, and punctuating thoughtfully. As a result, you make yourself understood and your views appreciated. You will become rich and famous and hang out with all the Beautiful People. Not really. But your life will have greater meaning because you influence people you may never meet with the clarity and power of your message. Who knows, you might even change the world.

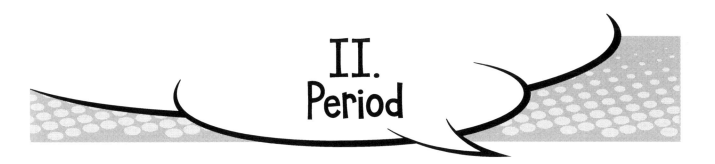

II.
Period

The most common punctuation tool is the period (.), a small dot with a big impact. Another word for the period is full-stop. You will use this mark more than any of the others. It shows the end of a sentence that contains both a subject and verb. It means stop here, dude. This thought is complete.

1. Belle prepared.

2. Belle prepared for the test.

These examples are **simple sentences**. The first includes only a subject and a verb: *Belle prepared.* The second contains a subject, verb, and a phrase containing the object: *Belle prepared for the test.* Sentences like these are straight roads. They contain no curves, constructions sites, or other holdups that slow you down until you arrive at the end. When you get there, the period says stop, dudette. You may be cool, but you're done here. Please move on to another thought.[8]

Yet what comprises a complete thought can be confusing for beginning writers. They often make the mistakes shown in examples #3 and #4.

3. Belle lost her math book. Which cost a lot of money.

The sentence *Belle lost her math book.* constitutes a complete thought and so the writer correctly ended it with a period. But the phrase *which had cost a lot of money* is not a sentence. A **phrase** consists of a few words expressing an idea, but it does not contain both a subject and verb. In this example, it adds information about the lost book. How should you fix this problem?

To fix example #3, you have at least three choices in your toolbox.

First, you might select a period and change the phrase into a sentence. *Belle lost her math **book. It** cost a lot of money.* By creating two short sentences, you add emphasis and tension.

Second, as I will explain in a few moments, you might express anger by inserting an

---

[8] I adapted the road metaphor from Roy Peter Clark, p. 46. When writers use metaphors, they take something you know and use it to explain something you don't know.

exclamation point at the end of the second sentence. *Belle lost her math book. It cost a lot of* **money!** Either the period or exclamation point might be effective in some paragraphs.

Third, you might select a comma and use it to create one sentence in which the parts are linked: *Belle lost her math* **book,** *which cost a lot of money.* This choice reads smoothly and might also be effective, depending on the point of your paragraph. The period, exclamation point, and comma are tools. **Tool-based punctuation teaches you that the choice depends on the context.**

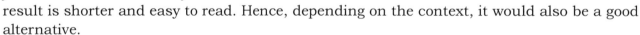

4. Belle found her math book, she feels better.

Example #4 contains two complete thoughts in one sentence. For this reason, you would not normally use a comma to link them together because the passage can be improved in other ways.

Your toolbox for improving example #4 contains at least five choices.

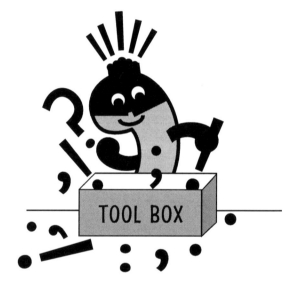

First, you might insert a period between them to create two simple sentences. *Belle found her math* **book.** *She feels better.* As above, if you read them out loud, the impact is choppy, bullet-like. In the context of the paragraph in which they appear, you might want this effect.

Second, you might insert an exclamation point, or even two. *Belle found her math* **book!** *She feels* **better!** Belle had spent hours looking for the lost tome. The marks express her relief, partly because you are no longer angry.

Third, you might insert the word *and.* You would also eliminate *she* as unnecessary. *Belle found her math book* **and** *feels better.* This result is shorter and easy to read. Hence, depending on the context, it would also be a good alternative.

I said you have five choices in your toolbox, right? As it turns out, you might also select either a colon or a semicolon to improve example #4. Both would be grammatically correct and effective in some paragraphs. For the moment, however, I am going to postpone the discussion of these options until later.

Did you notice that I did not provide you with a rule when discussing examples #3 and #4? **Tools are better than rules.** It is always easier to follow a rule. You don't have to think. And thinking is hard work, which most of us try to avoid. But rules cannot help you write sentences that express your intent clearly and concisely. A **tool-based approach,** by contrast, provides you with the choices needed to achieve these goals. This is why, in examples #3 and #4, I kept adding the comment *you might* in discussing your options.

So far, I have only suggested how to use the period, exclamation point, and comma. You employ these and the other tools to control the pace and meaning of your sentences and paragraphs. **The effective use of punctuation tools reflects your choices as a writer.** The word effective means to achieve a desired outcome. **The writer's goal must always be to create a positive experience for readers.** Otherwise, they will quit reading and you will have no impact on them. **Making effective choices requires judgment.** Those with judgment make wise decisions based on information, experience, or both. This development takes time and effort, of course. Reading this book and doing the worksheets are part of that process. In doing so, you will learn how to decide if and when to use punctuation tools to engage readers.

The period is the most common tool writers use to end sentences and, hence, the one most often seen by readers. Look at the pages of this book and see for yourself. But there are two other ways of creating a full-stop for readers: the question mark and exclamation point.

Your Notes Here

_____

_____

_____

_____

_____

_____

_____

_____

III. Question Mark

Like the period, the question mark (?) ends a sentence. Hence, this tool also tells readers to stop. Maybe that is why the symbol includes a period underneath the vertical hook. Other words for the question mark are interrogation point and query sign. The symbol, however, functions differently in speaking and writing.

In speaking, we ask others for information. Listeners know it's a question by the rising voice tone. You are invited, indeed, expected to reply. Not to do so would be rude.

In writing, however, the query sign serves as a **mark of reflection**. To reflect on a topic means to think about it, consider its implications, and perhaps to gain insight. When you read the title of this book, *Let's Eat Grandma?*, there was no need to or expectation of a reply. Rather, the title asks you to consider the question. What could it mean? Is it just absurd? What is its connection to the marvels of punctuation? The thought occurs: If you read the book, maybe the answer will appear. And it did.

5.   After finding her math book, did Belle prepare for the test?

When posing a question in social media, writers do expect an answer. Sometime. Not immediately. Perhaps after the reader thinks about it for awhile. One advantage of social media is that recipients can take time to consider the situation and compose a response. Thus, in this context the query sign still functions as a mark of reflection. When Belle's mother received the question in example #5, she did not have to respond right away. She could wait for a bit, observe Belle's behavior, and then reply. And when she did respond, it might express energy, passion, or emphasis.

Your Notes Here

_____

_____

_____

_____

_____

IV.
Exclamation Point

The exclamation point (!) provides a final tool for ending a sentence, but with emphasis.
This symbol also includes a period, located underneath the bang sign. In fact, Harry Shaw calls the exclamation point the "the period that blew its top."[9] This image aptly describes its purpose: to conclude by expressing surprise, relief, or any strong emotion. Thus, it can be a powerful tool.

You choose either the period or exclamation point depending on how much emphasis you wish to show. Most people don't blow their top very often, so the exclamation point occurs rarely in formal writing. This book provides an example. Look ahead and see how often you find this mark. Similarly, you would rarely use this mark in an essay for your teacher or a memo to your boss. In social media, however, people employ the exclamation point more often. In that context, Belle's mother might reply to my question in #5 in the following way:

> 6. Yes, Belle studied all night for the test!

I also use this mark much more often on social media. So I might reply with a single word:

> 7. Great!!!

Like the period and question mark, the exclamation point functions as a stop sign, a happy one in this case. When on social media, it provides an easy and brief way to express emotions, such as gratitude, thanks, appreciation, and pleasure. Of course, as mentioned when discussing the second choice in example #3, the exclamation point can also show anger. Having made this mistake and regretted it, I suggest not hitting the "send" key when you are annoyed. Wait one day. You'll be a happier person, so will the recipient, and the world will be a better place.

The problem with the exclamation point, whether in formal writing or social media, lies in its overuse. After a while, it loses impact. Moreover, as is so often the case, no rules can guide you. "Use the mark here but not there." "Use one mark here, two marks there, but never use three marks." Well, I just placed three marks in example #7. So what?

In writing, you're taught to compose complete sentences. They should always include, you're told, both a subject and a verb. *Well, not always.* People often talk in fragments. And sometimes you want your writing to mimic speaking. The rhetorical fragment provides a way.

---

[9] Harry Shaw, *Punctuate it Right!* (New York: Barnes & Noble, 1963), p. 94. It is unfortunate that this book is out of print.

V. Rhetorical Fragments

A rhetorical fragment consists of the intentional use of a word or phrase that stands by itself. The term rhetoric means to speak or write effectively. In formal writing, the rhetorical fragment varies the rhythm of a paragraph, often in interesting or compelling ways. For example, in the last paragraph on page 17 the rhetorical fragment *Well, not always* provides the transition point to introduce this section. In social media, the rhetorical fragment might be the entire message. Example #7, also on page 17, is a rhetorical fragment. I used exclamation points to produce a reaction in the reader, Belle's mother. But sometimes a period will do. Or even a question mark. Why not? Remember, however, that you need a stop sign to show the end of the thought. Pick the best tool, depending on the response you want to create.

You should use rhetorical fragments sparingly and, when you do, make sure they look intentional. In *A Wrinkle in Time,* Madeleine L'Engle illustrates their effective use. I have placed her rhetorical fragments in italics for easy identification.

> "IT was a brain. *A disembodied brain. An oversized brain, just enough larger than normal to be completely revolting and terrifying. A living brain. A brain that pulsed and quivered, that seized and commanded.* No wonder the brain was called IT."[10]

This passage does not include exclamation points. Rather, Ms. L'Engle uses periods to let the words create a frightening effect. In addition, she brackets the fragments with two short sentences. The resulting rhythm creates interest and suspense. Readers don't quit; they want to know more. They discover that IT is a powerful and evil force. IT wants to create a world where everyone is the same. IT argues that conformity leads to a perfect society in which everyone is happy. But will it? Readers become engaged. They want IT to be defeated because they know it's argument is wrong. You can achieve a similar reaction. Just imitate her.

As a beginner, you may think imitating her is impossible, or that writing well is beyond your reach. It is not, although the work demands an investment of your time.

You imitate her and improve your writing skills by considering everything you compose a first draft. Then rewriting it. That's what Ms. L'Engle did when she wrote *A Wrinkle in Time.* You may need to rewrite several times to discover your point. She also uses simple words, usually between one and three syllables, and active verbs. She composes short sentences, most often less than 20 words. She keeps her paragraphs short, too. Finally, as in this example, she uses punctuation tools effectively.

---

[10]Madeleine L'Engle, *A Wrinkle in Time* (New York: Farrar Straus and Giroux, 1962), p. 174.

Following these principles may not make you a best-selling author, but they will help you to write well. As a result, people will enjoy reading your work and you will influence them in some way.

The period, question mark, and explanation point function as stop signs. They tell readers that this thought is finished and now you are moving on to another one. Yet both the rhythm and meaning of each sentence depend on a set of internal punctuation tools: the comma, colon, and semi-colon. These marks tell readers to pause and then continue.

Your Notes Here

_____

_____

_____

_____

_____

_____

_____

_____

_____

_____

_____

_____

VI.
Comma

The comma (,) produces a slight separation in the parts of a sentence. Its appearance provides a clue to its purpose. The comma looks like a curved sewing needle used to hold pieces of fabric together. Its function in writing is similar: to hold sentences together. **Writers use the comma to introduce, join, insert, or link words or phrases in a sentence.** The marvel of the comma is that, when handled effectively, it makes your meaning clear. Conversely, of course, when omitted or inserted without thought, it can lead to a meaning you do not intend. Melanie discovered this possibility when she wrote "Let's eat Grandma."

Because it can be employed in so many ways, the comma is the second most widely used punctuation tool. One observer estimates that about 90% of all punctuation marks are either a period or a comma.[11] That figure may be low. Scan the next few paragraphs and notice that nearly all the marks are periods and commas. That pattern will continue throughout the book, even in the sections on colons and semicolons.

This frequency means that you can get along without using colons, semicolons, and the other marks. But without the comma, you cannot write clear, expressive, and meaningful sentences. Moreover, as Harry Shaw observes, once you learn to use the comma "no other mark can hold any terrors for you."[12] This relief occurs for two reasons: First, after learning to control the rhythm and meaning of a sentence with the comma, it becomes easier to add new marks to achieve the same goals. Second, as you will discover, use of the colon and semicolon often requires the comma, too. This is because your sentences become longer, more complex, and more satisfying to read. At least when done right.

When you write, **the slight separation signified by the comma tells your reader to slow down, to pause for a moment.** When placed effectively, this short breathing space affects the rhythm of a sentence. It moves along smoothly and readers enjoy the ride. They are also more likely to keep reading and remember what you have written.

These are your goals: for readers to take pleasure in what you have written and to have an impact on them. With a few exceptions, rules simply cannot help you achieve these

---

[11] David Crystal, p. 207.

[12] Harry Shaw, p. 64.

goals. Rather, you achieve them by **learning to use punctuation tools effectively.** Like any other skill, this process will take time and effort. You must learn to care about the comma. As you master its use, your life will be enriched as you influence others.

Your punctuation toolbox contains four types of commas. Each tool suggests that readers pause at a different point in the sentence.[13]

1. Introducer Comma

The first comma tool is the **introducer**: It appears after a word, phrase, or clause placed at the beginning of a sentence, before the subject or verb. It presents the sentence, telling readers there is more to come.

1. **Yes,** it is a good plan.

2. I will study for two **hours,** then watch the soccer match.

3. **Afterward,** I will get a good night's sleep.

As examples #1-3 suggest, introducer commas frequently appear after only a few words, which announce the rest of the sentence. But longer phrases followed by an introducer comma can also be effective.

4. After getting a good night's sleep and waking up **refreshed,** I awoke ready for the examination.

Although the opening clause in #4 comprises ten words, it leads readers to the point of the sentence rather easily. They understand why *I awoke ready for the examination.*

The trick when inserting an introducer comma is making sure that the pause creates a nice rhythm for the reader. This issue becomes especially important when you must decide whether or not to combine independent clauses into a compound sentence. An **independent clause** contains both a subject and verb and can stand alone as a sentence.

5. What is the difference between a cat and a comma? One has claws at the end of its **paws,** the other says to pause at the end of a clause.

Okay, it's a bad joke. But the punch line illustrates, once again, that **tools are better than rules**. A tool-based approach to the punch line recognizes that you have four choices, each of which is grammatically correct. Which one would you select?

---

[13] I took three of these names from Sheridan Baker, *The Practical Stylist*, 6th Edition (New York: Harper & Row, 1985), pp. 206-237. Dr. Baker calls one of his types the "connector comma," which I changed to the "joiner comma." Although out of print, this book remains available. It constitutes one of the best practical guides to effective writing.

First, as written, you might create a compound sentence by inserting an introducer comma. This choice produces a nice flow. But it is not the only reasonable option.

Second, instead of the introducer comma, you might insert a semicolon: *One has claws at the end of its **paws;** the other says to pause at the end of a clause.* As will be discussed later, the semicolon joins two ideas in one sentence; each is an independent clause. When a semicolon is used the pause becomes a bit longer. Think of a half-note instead of a quarter-note.

Third, you might omit the comma and insert *and: One has claws at the end of its **paws and the** other says to pause at the end of a clause.* By asking your readers not to pause, they sing-song through the punchline. This produces a nice effect.

Fourth, you might leave the punch line as two sentences separated by a period. *One has claws at the end of its paws. The other says to pause at the end of a clause.* This would usually be my least favorite choice. Although the full stop is often useful, depending on the context, the introductory clause and punchline comprise one topic. In most cases, your punctuation should show the connection.

Here is the lesson: **The tool you select should allow sentences to flow smoothly, both internally and when combined into paragraphs.** All your decisions about punctuation ought to reflect this goal. It's how you make reading a pleasure, thereby enriching the lives of your readers.

In addition to keeping the sentence flowing smoothly, you also need to make your meaning clear. Let's look at a different version of the sentence used as the title of this book.

> 6. Don't eat Grandma.

> 7. Don't **eat,** Grandma.

In these examples, you are the reader. Each contains an alert that you should attend to. In #6, the writer assumes you are a cannibal. A cannibal consumes human flesh and organs. You are being warned not to eat poor Grandma for lunch. It's more likely, of course, that Grandma wrote the note and made a small but important mistake. It is corrected in #7. Here Grandma left a note beside her apple pie and told you not to eat it. **One of the marvels of punctuation is that the introducer comma can affect the meaning of a sentence.** And the introducer comma is not alone. This lesson applies to all the tools discussed in this book.

But perhaps telling you not to eat the pie is not a strong enough message. Perhaps Grandma knows you like to pilfer whatever snack is available. Given this background, she can use other punctuation tools to convey her warning more forcefully. For example, she could substitute an exclamation point for the comma.

> 8. Don't **eat!** Grandma.

Now it's a command.

Although this example looks like Grandma wrote it on a post-it note placed next to the pie, the strategy is useful in other contexts. There is no reason you can't replace an introducer comma with an exclamation point or a question mark in formal writing. Doing so would depend on your purpose and what effect you want to achieve with your punctuation tools.

As the contents of your punctuation toolbox increase, many devices will become available. Your goal is to write clearly and effectively. In achieving this goal, I say rules, smules. **Smules** is a made-up word, called a neologism. I define smules as violating the rules for a reason, preferably a good one. This issue will come up again. For now, however, you should practice using the introducer comma.

Your Notes Here

_____

_____

_____

_____

_____

_____

_____

_____

_____

_____

_____

Place an introducer comma where appropriate **in the first sentence** in each example below. Extra spacing should give you room to write directly on this page. Suggested answers follow.

1. In 1969 Eric Carle had an idea for a children's book.[14]

2. Unfortunately he wanted to call it *The Very Hungry Caterpillar.*

3. As experts on grammar like to argue *very* is a weak and useless word. They say you should avoid it in your writing. This is probably good advice, at least most of the time.

4. Despite this argument Mr. Carle felt confident in his choice of this word for the title.

5. In the years since publication *The Very Hungry Caterpillar* sold over 30 million copies. Perhaps he was right.

6. In the story the caterpillar awakens one Sunday morning. He is hungry.

7. Although Mr. Carle did not give the caterpillar a name I always thought of him as Fred.

8. At first Fred ate a little bit each day.

9. For example he ate a piece of fruit on Monday. He was still hungry.

10. As each day passed Fred consumed a little more. But he remained hungry. Fred knew he must continue eating to discover his destiny.

11. Finally on Saturday Fred stuffed himself. He was no longer hungry.

12. As a result he had a stomach ache that evening.

13. On Sunday Fred ate a small green leaf and went to sleep.

14. After waking up he built himself a house. This house is called a cocoon.

15. After staying in the cocoon for more than two weeks Fred emerged as a beautiful butterfly. That was his destiny

16. Whatever you seek in life if you work hard and eat your veggies you can also become a beautiful butterfly and find your destiny.

---

[14] Eric Carle, *The Very Hungry Caterpillar* (New York: World Publishing Co, 1969). This is one of the most popular children's books ever written.

The word and comma in **boldface** show the suggested placement of the introducer comma. These recommendations might differ when the sentences are combined into a paragraph.

1. In **1969,** Eric Carle had an idea for a children's book.

2. **Unfortunately,** he wanted to call it *The Very Hungry Caterpillar.*

3. As experts on grammar like to **argue,** *very* is a weak and useless word. They say you should avoid it in your writing. This is probably good advice, at least most of the time.

4. Despite this **argument,** Mr. Carle felt confident in his choice of this word for the title.

5. In the years since **publication,** *The Very Hungry Caterpillar* sold over 30 million copies. Perhaps he was right.

6. In the **story,** the caterpillar awakens one Sunday morning. He is hungry.

7. Although Mr. Carle did not give the caterpillar a **name,** I always thought of him as Fred.

8. At **first,** Fred ate a little bit each day.

9. For **example,** he ate a piece of fruit on Monday. He was still hungry.

10. As each day **passed,** Fred consumed a little more. But he remained hungry. Fred knew he must continue eating to discover his destiny.

11. **Finally,** on Saturday Fred stuffed himself. He was no longer hungry

12. As a **result,** he had a stomach ache that evening.

13. On **Sunday,** Fred ate a small green leaf and went to sleep.

14. After waking **up,** he built himself a house. This house is called a cocoon.

15. After staying in the cocoon for more than two **weeks,** Fred emerged as a beautiful butterfly. That was his destiny.

16. Whatever you seek in **life,** if you work hard and eat your veggies you can also become a beautiful butterfly.

Comment: I like the pauses in each of these sentences. Try reading them out loud without the commas. But how about #16? Would you place a comma after *veggies,*? Although I chose not to, perhaps a pause at that point would be nice. Again, read it aloud and choose for yourself.

Notice that you can divide the worksheet into two paragraphs, say between #5 and #6. Here they are without the numbers:

> In **1969,** Eric Carle had an idea for a children's book. **Unfortunately,** he wanted to call it *The Very Hungry Caterpillar.* As experts on grammar like to **argue,** *very* is a weak and useless word. They say you should avoid it in your writing. This is probably good advice, at least most of the time. Despite this **argument,** Mr. Carle felt confident in his choice of this word for the title. In the years since **publication,** *The Very Hungry Caterpillar* sold over 30 million copies. Perhaps he was right.

> In the **story,** the caterpillar awakens one Sunday morning. He is hungry. Although Mr. Carle did not give the caterpillar a **name,** I always thought of him as Fred. At **first,** Fred ate a little bit each day. For **example,** he ate a piece of fruit on Monday. He was still hungry. As each day **passed,** Fred consumed a little more. But he remained hungry. He knew he must continue eating to discover his destiny. **Finally,** on Saturday Fred stuffed himself. He was no longer hungry. As a **result,** he had a stomach ache that evening. On **Sunday,** Fred ate a small green leaf and went to sleep. After waking **up,** he built himself a house. This house is called a cocoon. After staying in the cocoon for more than two **weeks,** Fred emerged as a beautiful butterfly. That was his desting. Whatever you seek in **life,** if you work hard and eat your veggies you can also become a beautiful butterfly.

Each paragraph deals with a different subject. The first focuses on the book's background. Actually, I have no idea about the background to *The Very Hungry Caterpillar.* I made it all up.

I made it up to pick a fight, possibly with your teachers. In *Elements of Style,* Mr. Strunk and Mr. White say to avoid "very" and other qualifying words (such as *little* boy or *pretty* day), describing them as "leeches that infest the pond of prose."[15] The word prose refers to written language. In other sections of their book, they tell you not to insert your own opinions and not to use inflated language. Like their phrase *leeches that infest the pond of prose?* Despite their overblown prose, limiting your use of meaningless qualifiers is a good idea. If, however, the qualifier is meaningful in the context, go for it. If you look ahead to Worksheet #3, I use "very" a couple of times. Rules, smules.

---

[15] Strunk and White, p. 73.

The second paragraph summarizes the story, which I did not make up. Some of the sentences in the second paragraph are a little short, perhaps too many. The result might feel too choppy as you read them. **It is always better to compose grammatically correct short sentences than mistake-filled long ones.** That said, you could solve this problem by creating a few compound sentences. The resulting combination of shorter and longer sentences might be easier on the reader.

Exercise: Although a worksheet can help. **You must practice.** Write 3-4 sentences about your favorite children's book using words or phrases offset by introducer commas in each. Alternatively, you might write 3-4 sentences about a time when you felt like you turned into a butterfly. Get a teacher or mentor to look at them and help you improve. You will make mistakes and it's okay. That's how you learn.

Write 3-4 sentences about either your favorite children's book OR when you felt like you turned into a butterfly.

Place an introducer comma where appropriate **in the first sentence** in each example below. Extra spacing should give you room to write directly on this page. Suggested answers follow.

1. In *The Giver* Lois Lowry tells the story of the Community from the point of view of eleven-year-old Jonas.[16]

2. Rejecting their past the citizens of the Community tried to create a utopia. A utopia is a perfect or ideal society.

3. In order to achieve this goal they eliminated all feelings and choices. Everyone got along and everyone was the same. The rulers organized social life to be as pleasant and convenient as possible. This was their idea of a utopia.

4. As the novel progresses Jonas makes many disturbing discoveries.

5. For example he discovers that when imperfect babies are "released" to preserve sameness they are murdered.

6. Similarly adults who fail to get along with others or break the rules are also "released."

7. For the reader the utopian appearance dissolves and the Community is revealed to be dystopian. A dystopian society is a repressive place in which the future looks bleak.

8. As the dreary life in the community becomes more apparent Jonas faces the Ceremony of Twelve. There he turns into an adult and receives his career assignment.

9. Surprisingly the rulers select Jonas to be the receiver of the community's memories. The Giver teaches Jonas all the memories of the community, good and bad.

---

[16] Lois Lowry, *The Giver* (Boston, MA: Houghton-Mifflin, 1993).

10. As a result Jonas learns to experience feelings. He feels anger, love, and other emotions that members of the community have suppressed.

11. In a society that has eliminated choice no one suffers from making poor decisions. They also do not experience the pleasure of making right decisions.

12. Over time Jonas comes to understand that people denied the ability to make choices can never be either happy or free.

13. After caring for and coming to love a baby named Gabriel Jonas discovers that Gabriel will be "released" soon. He is imperfect.

14. Still only twelve Jonas faces the first significant choice in his life.

15. In order to save Gabriel he must flee into the unknown and dangerous Elsewhere. He must find his destiny in a context of life and death.

16. By rescuing Gabriel and escaping the Community Jonas shows that he is willing to sacrifice his life for another. He becomes free to seek his destiny.

17. In addition the disruption in the Community forces its citizens to confront pleasure and pain again.

The word and comma in **boldface** show the suggested placement of the introducer comma. Again, these recommendations might differ when the sentences are combined into a paragraph.

1. In *The **Giver***, Lois Lowry tells the story of the Community from the point of view of eleven-year-old Jonas.

2. Rejecting their **past,** the citizens of the Community tried to create a utopia. A utopia is a perfect or ideal society.

3. In order to achieve this **goal,** they eliminated all feelings and choices. Everyone got along and everyone was the same. The rulers organized social life to be as pleasant and convenient as possible. This was their idea of a utopia.

4. As the novel **progresses,** Jonas makes many disturbing discoveries.

5. For **example,** he discovers that when imperfect babies are "released" to preserve sameness they are murdered.

6. **Similarly,** adults who fail to get along with others or break the rules are also "released."

7. For the **reader,** the utopian appearance dissolves and the Community is revealed to be dystopian. A dystopian society is a repressive place in which the future looks bleak.

8. As the dreary life in the community becomes more **apparent,** Jonas faces the Ceremony of Twelve. There he turns into an adult and receives his career assignment.

9. **Surprisingly,** the rulers select Jonas to be the receiver of the community's memories. The Giver teaches Jonas all the memories of the community, good and bad.

10. As a **result,** Jonas learns to experience feelings. He feels anger, love, and other emotions that members of the community have suppressed.

11. In a society that has eliminated **choice,** no one suffers from making poor decisions. They also do not experience the pleasure of making right decisions.

12. Over **time,** Jonas comes to understand that people denied the ability to make choices can never be either happy or free.

13. After caring for and coming to love a baby named **Gabriel,** Jonas discovers that Gabriel will be "released" soon. He is imperfect.[17]

14. Still only **twelve,** Jonas faces the first significant choice in his life.

15. In order to save **Gabriel,** he must flee into the unknown and dangerous Elsewhere. He must find his destiny in a context of life and death.

16. By rescuing Gabriel and escaping the **Community,** Jonas shows that he is willing to sacrifice his life for another. He becomes free to seek his destiny.

17. In **addition,** the disruption in the Community forces its citizens to confront pleasure and pain again.

Comment: The sentences in this worksheet are longer compared to the first one. Several of the introductory phrases are longer as well. In this context, would you omit some introducer commas or add a comma elsewhere? Number 5, for example, could be rewritten as follows: *For **example,** Jonas discovers that when imperfect babies are "released" to preserve **sameness,** they are murdered.* Adding a linker comma (discussed later) after *sameness,* also introduces another pause. My guess is that readers don't need it. What do you think?

Exercise: Write 3-4 sentences describing what a perfect society might look like. Alternatively, write 3-4 sentences discussing whether forcing people to confront pleasure and pain is a good thing. Use introducer commas in each sentence. Finally, combine the sentences in the worksheet into two or more paragraphs, each of which focuses on a different topic. Would your punctuation decisions change? I will discuss the logic of paragraph construction as we move along.

For now, just experiment to see what you come up with. Don't worry about mistakes. Learn from them.

---

[17] By the way, Gabriel reappears as an adult in a subsequent novel in the "Giver Quartet." See Lois Lowry, *Messenger* (Boston, MA: Houghton-Mifflin, 2004). In this set of four books, Ms. Lowry raises moral and political questions that people of all ages should consider.

Write a few sentences about either
A Perfect Society
OR
Whether forcing people to confront pain and pleasure is a good thing.

Now, combine the sentences above into two or more paragraphs, each of which focuses on a different topic. Would your punctuation decisions change?

2. Joiner Comma

The second comma tool is the **joiner.** It functions to join two sentences together to form a compound sentence. Recall that the two parts of the new sentence are called independent clauses.

1. She wants to be friends with **Jamelle.** She is hesitant.

2. She wants to be friends with **Jamelle,** yet is hesitant.

Both examples can be effective, depending on the context. Choosing #1 creates a short and distinct sound when read aloud. Choosing #2 produces a smoother sound. A **tool-based approach** says to make the choice based on what kind of rhythm you want in the paragraph as a whole.

Insertion of the word *yet* in #2 above is important. The joiner comma often (but not always) appears with the following seven **connecting words**: **f**or, **a**nd, **n**or, **b**ut, **o**r, **y**et, and **s**o. Grammarians call them **coordinating conjunctions**. They make it easy to join either two independent clauses with a comma or two simple alternatives without a comma.

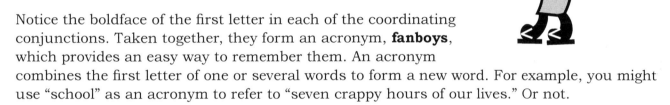

Notice the boldface of the first letter in each of the coordinating conjunctions. Taken together, they form an acronym, **fanboys**, which provides an easy way to remember them. An acronym combines the first letter of one or several words to form a new word. For example, you might use "school" as an acronym to refer to "seven crappy hours of our lives." Or not.

I asked one of my best students, eighteen-year-old Brenda, to compose a paragraph using each of the fanboys in order. She chose the problem of how to become friends with Jamelle, mentioned in examples #1 and #2 above, and wrote the following:

> I go to the gym every Saturday afternoon, **f**or I love to walk on the treadmill and then get some juice. Actually, I go to the gym to walk on the treadmill **a**nd watch the shirtless boys play basketball. I don't go to the gym for the exercise **n**or for the juice. I just like watching the basketball. Basketball is entertaining from the stands, **b**ut it's better up close where you can see the contact. Also, the boys usually choose teams: shirts **o**r skins. I sometimes think about going to the library instead, **y**et I always end up back at the gym. I've become friends with Jamelle, **s**o now I watch him play each week without sweating on the treadmill.

Although some unusual wording occurs due to my instructions, the boldface letters show that each coordinating conjunction appears in order. Brenda's cleverly constructed paragraph thus provides a way to discuss using, or not using, punctuation tools with each of the fanboys.

3. I go to the gym every Saturday **afternoon, for** I love to walk on the treadmill and then get some juice.

In this example, the two independent clauses can stand alone. *I go to the gym every Saturday afternoon. I love to walk on the treadmill and then get some juice.* But the hard stop is probably too abrupt, especially in the context of the entire paragraph. Inserting the joiner comma and the connecting word *for* creates a compound sentence that reads more smoothly. In this case, *for* describes the reason for going to the gym.

Brenda was constrained by the need to use *for* to begin her paragraph. Sheridan Baker argues, however, that *for* is the weakest coordinating conjunction.[18] It's a way of saying *because*, a stronger term. You can often substitute *because* into the sentence without loss of meaning. In this case, you can also eliminate the joiner comma: I *go to the gym every Saturday afternoon **because** I love to walk on the treadmill and then get some juice.* This version reads smoothly and expresses her meaning more directly. Both word and comma choice often reflect the writer's judgment about how to create a good experience for the reader.

4. Actually, I go to the gym to walk on the treadmill **and** watch the shirtless boys play basketball.

Now the truth about Brenda's motives comes out! She uses the adverb, *actually* and an introducer comma to open the sentence. In this context, it means "the truth is." This admission is followed by two independent clauses. Each of them could stand as separate sentences. *I go to the gym to walk on the treadmill. I watch the shirtless boys play basketball.* (In example #4, the second *I* is implied and omitted.) The conjunction *and* adds items together when inserted. Although the sentence is a bit long, 21 words, it reads easily without a joiner comma. Reread it out loud with and without a pause, and decide for yourself whether it needs this tool. Reasonable people might disagree. Remember your goal: using punctuation tools to create a positive experience for the reader.

5. I don't go to the gym for the exercise **nor** for the juice. I just like watching the basketball.

I just like watching the basketball. Really Brenda? Anyway, in this example *nor* adds a negative rationale to the previous negative *don't.* The sentence probably does not require a joiner comma because the final phrase, *for the juice,* does not contain either a subject or verb. Again, you might disagree. But remember, both here and in earlier examples, **the tool you do not use is as important as the one you do.**

6. Basketball is entertaining from the **stands, but** it's better up close where you can see the contact.

---

[18] Sheridan Baker, p. 209.

It turns out that Brenda knows basketball. It is a contact sport, best appreciated when you sit near the court. Grammatically, this compound sentence probably needs the joiner comma due to the contrasting subject of the two independent clauses. The use of *but* shows that difference and provides an easy transition.

7. Also, the boys usually choose teams: shirts **or** skins.

When males play pickup basketball, members of one team will sometimes take off their shirts so that players can distinguish teammates from opponents. Brenda wisely inserted a forward-looking colon in front of the phrase *shirts or skins* to add punch to the sentence. In addition to creating interest, the forward-looking colon works effectively in the context of the paragraph. The use of *or* presents the players on each side. Inserting a comma in front of *or*, with its slight pause, would be awkward. Read it aloud both ways and you will see this.

8. I sometimes think about going to the library **instead, yet** I always end up back at the gym.

Remember, Brenda is a good student. Saturday afternoon constitutes her leisure time. This example provides another illustration of how a compound sentence uses one of the fanboys connecting words: *I sometimes think about going to the library instead. I always end up back at the gym.* The use of *yet* suggests an alternative outcome. When combined with the joiner comma, the result eliminates the awkward full stop.

9. I've become friends with **Jamelle, so** now I watch him play each week without sweating on the treadmill.

What a nice outcome. This final example again displays two independent clauses: *I've become friends with Jamelle. Now I watch him play each week without sweating on the treadmill.* You might think that separating the clauses with a period makes the reading too choppy. Inserting *Jamelle, so* shows how the result of being friends with Jamelle changes Brenda's behavior. As with previous examples, using the joiner comma to create a compound sentence may be easier to read.

Before continuing, let's consider Brenda's paragraph as a whole. **The ideal paragraph focuses on a single topic.** It does not matter how long the paragraph is. It can be one sentence, five, or any length at all. In her case, while the paragraph appears to center on watching the boys play basketball, it turns out to be about her relationship with Jamelle. This little twist at the end adds surprise, which is always effective. In addition, except for #6, Brenda used active verbs in every sentence. They add punch and create interest.

Now observe the logical construction of Brenda's paragraph. It's really pretty skillful. Please reread the original paragraph out loud, this time looking for the pattern. Here it is again.

> I go to the gym every Saturday afternoon, for I love to walk on the treadmill
> and then get some juice. Actually, I go to the gym to walk on the treadmill and
> watch the shirtless boys play basketball. I don't go to the gym for the exercise
> nor for the juice. I just like watching the basketball. Basketball is entertaining

from the stands, but it's better up close where you can see the contact. Also, the boys usually choose teams: shirts or skins. I sometimes think about going to the library instead, yet I always end up back at the gym. I've become friends with Jamelle, so now I watch him play each week without sweating on the treadmill.

I hope you noticed that the first sentence introduces her topic: going to the gym. Then she elaborates on her motives in the middle section, which turn out to be mixed. She creates interest by misleading the reader and then revealing her main topics, watching basketball and the boys. Finally, she brings the paragraph home with an unexpected closing sentence. The strong conclusion marks a good paragraph, the kind you're taught to construct.

Later on, I will look at how beginners can use punctuation tools effectively in the context of writing well-organized paragraphs. For now, however, it is time to practice what you have just learned.

Your Notes Here

_____

_____

_____

_____

_____

_____

_____

_____

_____

_____

_____

Place a joiner comma if and where appropriate **in the first sentence** in each example below. Extra spacing should give you room to write directly on this page. If the first sentence seems correct as written, however, place a letter C next to it. Suggested answers follow.

1. Nicolas proposed we cook alligator stew but the other children made barf noises.[19]

2. Kevin informed them that they can choose to eat alligator stew or fried grasshoppers.

3. Neither alligator stew nor fried grasshoppers satisfied ten-year-old Richard.

4. He wanted to eat Twinkies but everyone ignored him. They are not healthy.

5. Both alligator stew and fried grasshoppers are healthy to eat yet many chefs prefer the stew.

6. We discussed the matter and could not decide so we voted.

7. Some people find democracy to be frustrating but we made a difficult decision without fighting. We chose the alligator stew.

8. Cooking the alligator took a long time because it was very large.

9. We sautéed the meat with butter and garlic yet it wasn't ready to eat. Cooks sauté food by browning it in a skillet with oil or butter. The word sauté is pronounced "sawtay."

10. We then heated the meat in a large pot with garlic and tomato sauce but the dish still needed something else

11. Nicolas suggested salt and pepper but Alexis thought some cream would be better. We added both.

12. I hated wasting a single drop of the stew for it was expensive to catch and kill the alligator. It was also time consuming to make for dinner.

13. My dog Luna refused to eat her dog food nor would she touch a saucer of the alligator stew.

14. Luna continued to ignore her serving of stew so I got a fork and ate it myself. I did not barf.

---

[19] Andrew Zimmern, *Andrew Zimmern's Field Guide to Exceptionally Weird, Wild, Wonderful Foods* (New York: Fiewel and Friends, 2012). Mr. Zimmern describes both dishes mentioned here, but not the Twinkies.

The word and comma in **boldface** show the suggested placement of the joiner comma. In some cases, use of the joiner comma may be optional, depending on the rhythm of the sentence. Also, these recommendations might differ when the sentences are combined into one or more paragraphs.

1. Nicolas proposed we cook alligator **stew,** but the other children made barf noises.

2. Kevin informed them that they can choose to eat alligator stew or fried grasshoppers.

3. Neither alligator stew nor fried grasshoppers satisfied ten-year-old Richard.

4. He wanted to eat **Twinkies,** but everyone ignored him. They are not healthy.

5. Both alligator stew and fried grasshoppers are healthy to **eat,** yet many chefs prefer the stew.

6. We discussed the matter and could not **decide,** so we voted.

7. Some people find democracy to be **frustrating,** but we made a difficult decision without fighting. We chose the alligator stew.

8. Cooking the alligator took a long time because it was very large.

9. We sautéed the meat with butter and **garlic,** yet it wasn't ready to eat. Cooks sauté food by browning it in a skillet with oil or butter. The word sauté is pronounced "sawtay."

10. We then heated the meat in a large pot with garlic and tomato **sauce,** but the dish still needed something else

11. Nicolas suggested salt and **pepper,** but Alexis thought some cream would be better. We added both.

12. I hated wasting a single drop of the **stew,** for it was expensive to catch and kill the alligator. It was also time consuming to make for dinner.

13. My dog Luna refused to eat her dog **food,** nor would she touch a saucer of the alligator stew.

14. Luna continued to ignore her serving of **stew,** so I got a fork and ate it myself. I did not barf.

Comment: There are no joiner commas in #2 & #3, since they seem to read smoothly. Do you agree? In #8, I chose *because* instead of the weaker word "for." I view the joiner comma as optional in #13-14. Your writing should establish an easy rhythm. Do you want readers to pause when "hearing" the last two examples?

Exercise: Write 3-4 sentences about the strangest food your father or mother ever cooked. Use joiner commas in each. In addition, you might go back to Worksheet #1 and rewrite it in paragraph form, this time composing compound sentences with joiner commas. Finally, the sentences in the worksheet could be divided into, say, two paragraphs, each dealing with a different subject. For example, sentences #1-7 focus on the decision about what to cook. By contrast, sentences #8-14 describe cooking and eating the alligator. Considered in these two contexts, would your punctuation decisions change? Play with different alternatives. Don't worry about making mistakes.

Write 3-4 sentences about the strangest food your mother or father ever cooked.

Insert a joiner comma if and where appropriate **in the first sentence** in each example below. Extra spacing should give you room to write directly on this page. If the first sentence is correct as written, however, place a letter C next to it. Suggested answers follow. **Warning:** Not all these sentences use one of the fanboys as a connecting word.

1. He was harvested from a cow but Matteo Alacrán grew into a normal human being. Or did he? This shocking scene occurs in the opening pages of *The House of the Scorpion*, a novel set in the not too distant future.[20]

2. Matteo is a clone of the drug lord El Patrón who is also named Matteo Alacrán. A clone is an exact genetic copy of the individual from which it is derived.

3. El Patrón wishes to live forever so Matteo is only the most recent clone destined to be used for body parts.

4. People treat Matteo like an animal for he lives solely to provide organs for El Patrón.

5. Alacrán means scorpion in Spanish so images of scorpions appear throughout the vast estate. They frighten people who enter it.

6. The estate consists of a strip of land between Mexico and the United States which means immigrants seeking freedom and opportunity must cross it to get to the United States.

7. The Farm Patrol captures people attempting this journey and transforms them into eejits by inserting computer chips into their brains. Eejit is an Irish word meaning idiot.

8. El Patrón seeks wealth and power and he uses the chips to keep eejits enslaved.

9. The eejits grow poppies and transform them into opium which is sold to addicts around the world.

---

[20] Nancy Farmer, *The House of the Scorpion* (New York: Atheneum Books for Young Readers, 2002). Although intended for adolescents, Ms. Farmer deals with timeless ethical and political dilemmas of interest to people of all ages.

10. Matteo escapes from the Alacrán estate but he is imprisoned again and forced to work on a plankton farm with other lost boys. In this dystopian future, plankton serves as a source of food for many people. Plankton is a small sea animal.

11. Matteo overcomes his fear and leads a breakout because he wants to free the eejits and destroy the drug trade.

12. Matteo has five fingers and displays empathy for others yet people believe he is not human. Are they correct?

13. Immigrants deserve to be jailed or exploited since they have broken the law. Or do they? Is there a higher law?

The word and comma in **boldface** show the suggested placement of the joiner comma. In some cases, use of the joiner comma may be optional, depending on the flow you wish to establish. As always, these recommendations might differ when the sentences are combined into a paragraph.

1. He was harvested from a **cow,** but Matteo Alacrán grew into a normal human being. Or did he? This shocking scene occurs in the opening pages of *The House of the Scorpion,* a novel set in the not too distant future.

2. Matteo is a clone of the drug lord El **Patrón,** who is also named Matteo Alacrán. A clone is an exact genetic copy of the individual from which it is derived.

3. El Patrón wishes to live **forever,** so Matteo is only the most recent clone destined to be used for body parts.

4. People treat Matteo like an **animal,** for he lives solely to provide organs for El Patrón.

5. Alacrán means scorpion in **Spanish,** so images of scorpions appear throughout the vast estate. They frighten people who enter it.

6. The estate consists of a strip of land between Mexico and the United **States,** which means immigrants seeking freedom and opportunity must cross it to get to the United States.

7. The Farm Patrol captures people attempting this **journey,** and transforms them into eejits by inserting computer chips into their brains. Eejit is an Irish word meaning idiot.

8. El Patrón seeks wealth and **power,** and he uses the chips to keep eejits enslaved.

9. The eejits grow poppies and transform them into **opium,** which is sold to addicts around the world.

10. Matteo escapes from the Alacrán **estate,** but he is imprisoned again and forced to work on a plankton farm with other lost boys. In this dystopian future, plankton serves as a source of food for many people. Plankton is a small sea animal.

11. Matteo overcomes his fear and leads a **breakout** because he wants to free the eejits and destroy the drug trade.

12. Matteo has five fingers and displays empathy for **others,** yet people believe he is not human. Are they correct?

13. Immigrants deserve to be jailed or **exploited,** since they have broken the law. Or do they? Is there a higher law?

Comment: I chose to insert a joiner comma in #6. Do you agree? It's rather long at 29 words. Would it be more effective to divide it into two sentences? Number 10 is also long at 24 words. Does it read smoothly? Or would you break it up by inserting a period? Number 11 seems to have a nice rhythm without a joiner comma after *because*. Do you agree? These kinds of a judgment calls occur with nearly every sentence.

Exercise: Write 3-4 sentences about the potential significance of cloning. Would you eat a cloned pig? Is a human being cloned from an American citizen also entitled to U.S. citizenship? Alternatively, write about the American treatment of immigrants. Do we apply the law strictly or change it? What, if any, religious values should affect these decisions? Use joiner commas in each sentence. Finally, the sentences in the worksheet could be divided into three or perhaps four paragraphs. Where would you make the cuts? Why? And would your punctuation decisions change?

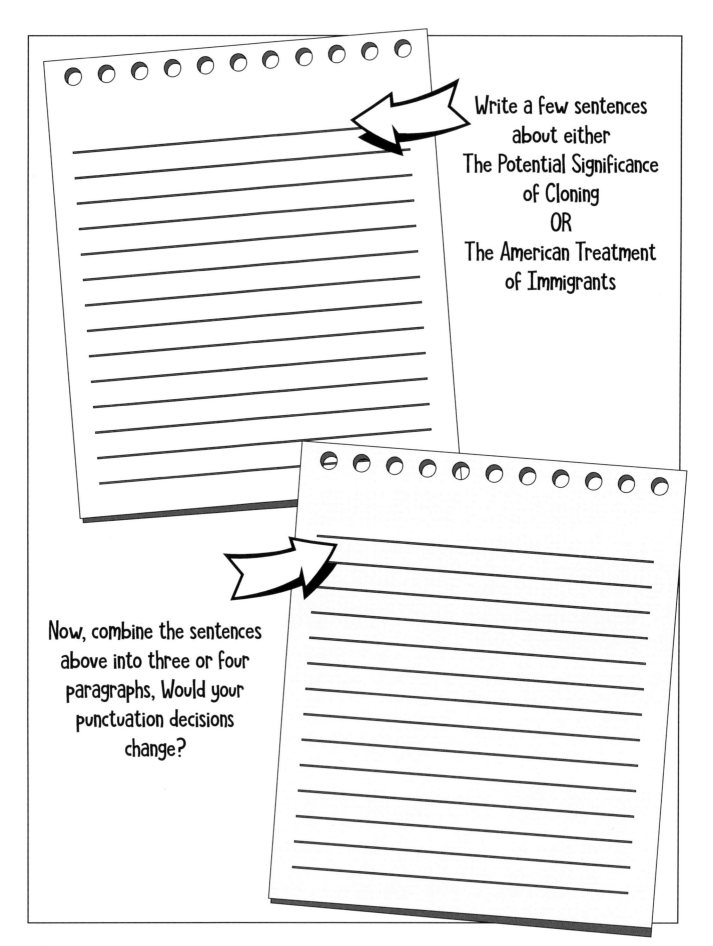

Write a few sentences about either
The Potential Significance
of Cloning
OR
The American Treatment
of Immigrants

Now, combine the sentences above into three or four paragraphs, Would your punctuation decisions change?

3. Inserter Commas

Inserter commas allow writers to place an explanatory phrase into the middle of a sentence. *It's a sidebar comment that adds information but, if omitted, still leaves the sentence intact and its pace comfortable.* Inserter commas come in pairs. They tie off the inserted phrase, one in front and one after.

The italicized sentence in the paragraph above provides an example. Read these two versions of it aloud, listening for the difference.

1. It's a sidebar comment that adds information but**, if omitted,** still leaves the sentence intact and its pace comfortable.

2. It's a sidebar comment that adds information but still leaves the sentence intact and its pace comfortable.

The inserter commas bracket the sidebar, *if omitted,* in #1. Removing the phrase in #2, however, does no harm to the sentence. It still makes perfect sense.

Here are two more examples that anticipate the topic of the next worksheet:

3. The Ashanti **people,** who live in **Ghana,** tell stories about a spider-god named Anansi.

4. He is a **hero,** despite his small **size,** because he triumphs over more powerful foes.

Again, the inserter commas tie off the sidebars. Reread the examples with them removed: *The Ashanti people tell stories about a spider-god named Anansi. He is a hero because he triumphs over more powerful foes.* Although the sentences stand alone, the incidental comments provide readers with more information without disrupting the flow of the sentence.

Just as both introducer and joiner commas can influence the meaning of a sentence, so can inserter commas. **Only create the sidebar, and bracket it with inserter commas, when it refers to a particular topic.** Read the examples below aloud and listen for the difference.[21]

5. My grandma who runs marathons is ninety.

6. My **grandma,** who runs **marathons,** is ninety.

How many grandmothers do you have in #5 and how many in #6? It's a trick question. To answer it, you must determine whether the phrase *who runs marathons* refers to a general category of people, one of several grandmas, or a particular person, your one and only grandma.

---

[21]Adapted from Sheridan Baker, p. 211. Grammarians refer to restrictive clauses (#5) and nonrestrictive clauses (#6).

Many children live in blended families and enjoy the presence of three or even four grandparents. In #5, the focus is on your several grandmas, only one of whom runs marathons. In this case, the sentence does not require inserter commas. More generally, if you're referring to a general category of topics inserter commas are not needed to make the meaning clear.

Now reread #6 without the sidebar created by inserter commas: *My grandmother is ninety.* Stated this way, it becomes obvious that you have only one grandma and she is the focus of the sentence. In this case, the phrase *who runs marathons* is not essential to its meaning. Including it, however, adds interesting information about her athletic accomplishments. More generally, if you're referring to a particular topic, it's a sidebar. Use a pair of inserter commas to tie it off from the rest of the sentence.

One caution before turning to the worksheets: Sidebar comments placed in the middle of a sentence can disrupt its flow. Remember you are using punctuation tools to engage readers. **When you insert an explanatory word or phrase be sure that the result maintains an easy rhythm.** I continue emphasizing the importance of rhythm for two reasons. First, smoothly written sentences and paragraphs are easier to read. Second, readers remember what you are saying more easily. After you do the next worksheet, will you remember what escargots are? Do you want to try them?

Your Notes Here

_____

_____

_____

_____

_____

_____

_____

_____

Place a pair of inserter commas around the sidebar or sidebars **in the first sentence** in each example below. Extra spacing should give you room to write directly on this page. If the first sentence flows smoothly as written, however, place a letter C (for correct) next to it. Suggested answers follow.

1. We left the house yesterday around 5:00 pm to go to the restaurant.

2. The valet who wore a red vest parked our car. A valet performs personal services. You say valet as "vellay," with emphasis on the second syllable.

3. We had to wait it seemed like forever before being seated.

4. The server however came quickly to our table and after explaining the menu took our orders.

5. I ordered escargots which are snails as an appetizer. You say escargots as if the "t" is not there: "escargoes." An appetizer is a small dish served before the main meal.

6. The escargots arrived smothered in butter and garlic.

7. My friend Alan who is only fourteen was afraid to try them.

8. But my friend Liliana also fourteen and braver than Alan immediately took one.

9. She then took another and between bites pronounced them delicious.

10. Although the escargots cost a lot of money about $15 they were worth every penny.

The phrase in **boldface and the accompanying inserter commas** show their suggested placement. In some cases, use of inserter commas may be optional, depending on the flow you wish to establish. As always, these recommendations might differ when the sentences are combined into a paragraph.

1. We left the house **yesterday, around 5:00 pm,** to go to the restaurant.

2. The **valet, who wore a red vest,** parked our car. A valet performs personal services. You say valet as "vellay," with emphasis on the second syllable.

3. We had to **wait, it seemed like forever,** before being seated.

4. The **server, however,** came quickly to our table **and, after explaining the menu,** took our orders.

5. I ordered **escargots, which are snails,** as an appetizer. You say escargots as if the "t" is not there: "escargoes." An appetizer is a small dish served before the main meal.

6. The escargots arrived smothered in butter and garlic.

7. My friend **Alan, who is only fourteen,** was afraid to try them.

8. But my friend **Liliana, also fourteen and braver than Alan,** immediately took one.

9. She then took another **and, between bites,** pronounced them delicious.

10. Although the escargots cost a lot of **money, about $15,** they were worth every penny.

Comment: You could get away without the inserter commas in #1. Are there other examples in which the commas could be omitted? Or perhaps one of the sidebars should be either taken out as irrelevant or rewritten in a separate sentence? Remember your goal: A smooth rhythm.

Exercise: Write 3-4 sentences about your favorite restaurant using inserter commas in each. Would you divide the sentences in this worksheet into two paragraphs? If so, where? And why? If you did this, would your punctuation decisions change?

Write 3-4 sentences about your favorite restaurant.

Now, divide the sentences above into two paragraphs. Do your punctuation decisions change?

Place a pair of inserter commas around the sidebar **in the first sentence** in each example below. Extra spacing should give you room to write directly on this page. If the first sentence flows smoothly as written, however, place a letter C (for correct) next to it. Suggested answers follow.

1. People pass down their traditional stories and beliefs sometimes called folktales from one generation to another by word of mouth.

2. But long ago according to the Ashanti people there were no stories in the world. Nyame the sky-god possessed all the stories and kept them to himself.[22]

3. Anansi who was just a spider asked Nyame how much it would cost to buy the stories. Nyame told Anansi to bring back Onini, the Python, Osebo, the Leopard, and the Mboro hornets.

4. How could a small arachnid another name for a spider perform these difficult tasks?

5. Anansi thought about the problem discarded several ideas and developed a plan.

6. Onini the Python wanted to know how long he was. Onini was also not very smart.

7. The only way to solve this problem Anansi suggested was to tie Onini to a branch and measure him. Onini agreed. Having deceived Onini, Anansi took the bound-up snake to Nyame.

8. Anansi dug a hole covered it with sticks and straw and waited for Osebo the Leopard. Osebo fell into the hole and had to be rescued.

9. Anansi used his spider-webs which were very strong to lift Osebo out of the hole. Having tricked Osebo, Anansi took the bound-up leopard to Nyame.

10. Anansi suggested to the Mboro hornets that they hide from the rain in an empty gourd and when they obliged he sealed the opening. After fooling and capturing the hornets, Anansi took them to Nyame.

11. These results pleased Nyame and upon receiving the last payment he gave Anansi all the stories.

12. The folk stories of West Africa called Anansi Tales now belong to all the people in the world.

---

[22] The Anansi stories are folktales that originated in Ghana and spread to the Americas. Many authors have retold various versions. I base the worksheet on one written by Verna Aardema, *Anansi Does the Impossible* (New York: Aladdin Paperbacks, 2000).

The phrase in **boldface** shows the suggested placement of the inserter commas. In some cases, their use may be optional, depending on the flow you wish to establish. As always, these recommendations might differ when the sentences are combined into a paragraph.

1. People pass down their traditional stories and **beliefs, sometimes called folktales**, from one generation to another by word of mouth.

2. But long **ago, according to the Ashanti people,** there were no stories in the world. Nyame the sky-god possessed all the stories and kept them to himself.

3. **Anansi, who was just a spider,** asked Nyame how much it would cost to buy the stories. Nyame told Anansi to bring back Onini, the Python, Osebo, the Leopard, and the Mboro hornets.

4. How could a small **arachnid, another name for a spider,** perform these difficult tasks?

5. Anansi thought about the **problem, discarded several ideas,** and developed a plan.

6. **Onini, the Python,** wanted to know how long he was. Onini was also not very smart.

7. The only way to solve this **problem, Anansi suggested,** was to tie Onini to a branch and measure him. Onini agreed. Having deceived Onini, Anansi took the bound-up snake to Nyame.

8. Anansi dug a **hole, covered it with sticks and straw,** and waited for Osebo the Leopard. Osebo fell into the hole and had to be rescued.

9. Anansi used his spider-**webs, which were very strong,** to lift Osebo out of the hole. Having tricked Osebo, Anansi took the bound-up leopard to Nyame.

10. Anansi suggested to the Mboro hornets that they hide from the rain in an empty gourd **and, when they obliged,** he sealed the opening. After fooling and capturing the hornets, Anansi took them to Nyame.

11. These results pleased Nyame **and, upon receiving the last payment**, he gave Anansi all the stories.

12. The folk stories of West **Africa, called Anansi Tales,** now belong to all the people in the world.

Comment: Although I suggest using inserter commas in each of these examples, what do you think? Reread them out loud with and without the sidebars. Would you take out one of them or perhaps rewrite it as a separate sentence?

Exercise: Write 3-4 sentences about a folktale you know using inserter commas in each. Alternatively, write 3-4 sentences about Fred, the *Very Hungry Caterpillar,* using inserter commas in each.

Your toolbox now contains three comma tools: the introducer, joiner, and inserters. It also holds three full-stop tools: the period, question mark, and exclamation point. Consider dividing the sentences in this worksheet into two or more paragraphs and using all your punctuation tools to establish a better rhythm. Try several different ways. Don't be afraid of errors. Rules, smules.

Write 3-4 sentences about a folktale you know using inserter commas in each.

Alternatively, write 3-4 sentences about Fred, the *Very Hungry Caterpillar,* using inserter commas in each.

4. Linker Comma

The **linker** comma usually appears near the end of a sentence and serves three purposes. Each one links, or connects, the later part of a sentence to the earlier part.

First, the linker comma identifies or renames a noun or pronoun.

> 1. Carla phoned her **tutor,** Leonard.
>
> 2. She has another name for **him,** the Old Man.

In these examples, each sentence works without the additional identifying noun or pronoun. *She phoned her tutor. She has another name for him.* Identifying the noun or pronoun provides more information to the reader in a simple, easy to read fashion. Without the pause, the examples would not read so smoothly.

Second, the linker comma connects an afterthought to a sentence. The afterthought explains or adds to what came before.

> 3. Carla and her friends stayed for the entire **game,** which ended late.
>
> 4. Carla finished the book after arriving **home,** although it bored her to tears.
>
> 5. Carla would rather have gone to **bed,** but reading the book was a school assignment.

Once again, each sentence makes perfect sense without a postscript. *Carla and her friends stayed for the entire game. Carla finished the book after arriving home. Carla would rather have gone to bed.* But in each case, the linker comma introduces a phrase to the sentence that provides additional information.

It is possible, of course, to convert any of these examples into two separate sentences. Consider #3: *Carla and her friends stayed the entire game. It ended late.* Of course, what's going on around these two short sentences is important. In the context of the paragraph as a whole, this construction might be effective. In many cases, however, inserting a comma and an afterthought creates a smoother read.

In examples #3-5, adding the linker comma does not influence the meaning of the sentence. The afterthought simply provides more information. In some cases, however, the pause signified by the linker comma changes the meaning in a subtle way. A subtle distinction seems small but turns out to be important.

> 6. Carla granted the usual permission and walked away.
>
> 7. Carla granted the usual **permission,** and walked away.[23]

---

[23] Examples #6 and #7 are taken from Sheridan Baker, p. 208.

The meaning of each example differs depending on whether you insert a linker comma. Without it, #6 implies that this event is normal, of little consequence. Think carefully about #7, however, and read it aloud: *Carla granted the usual **permission,** and walked away.* The insertion of the linker comma, with its little pause, makes the last phrase an afterthought. In so doing, it suggests a negative attitude on Carla's part. Is she irritated? You would need to see the sentence embedded in its paragraph to know.

> 8. Carla became ill and went home.

> 9. Carla became **ill,** and went home.

Again, the meaning of each example differs slightly without and with the linker comma. In #8, she went home immediately. In #9, however, the meaning of the sentence changes in a subtle way when the linker comma creates an afterthought. It suggests a literal pause, a passage of time. She became ill and later she went home.

Notice that rules cannot dictate your decisions. A **tool-based approach**, however, emphasizes that you have choices and that these choices have consequences. Use the linker comma carefully, with attention to its implications.

Third, the linker comma connects items in a series of three.

> 10. Will Carla cook steaks, hamburgers, or hot dogs for dinner?

> 11. If she does, will they be made from cows, dogs, or cats?

Whoa! Food from dogs or cats? We'll come back to that issue. For now, let's consider the implications of three items in a series.

Speakers, writers, and artists often use "the rule of three" to communicate effectively. Roy Peter Clark suggests that this is because "three provides a sense of the whole" in our culture, a feeling of completeness.[24] I suppose that's as good an explanation as any.

The problem is how to punctuate a series of three items, whether they be words, phrases, or clauses. Notice in examples #10 and #11 that the coordinating conjunction *or* follows the comma. The word *and* can also be used for the same purpose.

As David Crystal observes, grammarians disagree about placing a comma in front of the coordinating conjunction in a series of three.[25] Most Americans say to use it all the time.

---

[24] Roy Peter Clark, p. 100.

[25] David Crystal describes the disagreement on pp. 250-258. The comma placed before "and" in a list is often called the Oxford Comma. The name comes from its use by editors at the Oxford University Press in England. You can track the argument by looking up "Oxford Comma" with your search engine. Even a rock band, Vampire Weekend, joined the dispute in their song, "The Oxford Comma." Believe it or not, this song was a hit. They ask, in strong language, who cares about the oxford comma. As you will see, Carla does. And maybe you should.

Most British observers say not to use it, unless it is needed to make your meaning clear. As shown in the examples above and elsewhere in this book. I always place a comma before the connecting word introducing the last item.

Whatever style you choose, be consistent. If your teacher claims your style is wrong, don't give in. Defend yourself! But be careful. Just like the other comma tools, inserting or not inserting a linker comma can affect your meaning.

> 12. Carla likes cooking dogs and cats.

Without any commas, the objects of the sentence, *cooking dogs and cats,* all have equal emphasis. Read the sentence out loud with no pauses. It says that Carla claims to like cooking dogs and cats. Really? Is she going to eat them medium rare or well done? Should I be worried about my pets? If you read #12 as written, these questions follow logically.

Let's rewrite the example to see if these questions can be avoided. This time the British way will be followed.

> 13. Carla likes **cooking,** dogs and cats.

You might read this sentence differently, but it still seems to me that she wants to cook and then eat dogs and cats. Maybe I should still be worried about my pets. *Carla likes cooking, especially dogs and cats.* With the addition of *especially,* you see the equivalence of *dogs and cats.* They refer back to *cooking.* Do you think this is what she means? Perhaps the writer is still not being clear. Perhaps the American way of placing the comma in front of *and* shows young Carla's intent more accurately.

> 14. Carla likes **cooking, dogs, and** cats.

Now the meaning becomes crystal clear: When the linker comma precedes *and* all the objects receive equal emphasis. As a result, we now know that three distinct pleasures fill Carla's life: cooking, dogs, and cats. It looks like my pets will survive. Their survival reflects the intentional use of the linker comma to say precisely what is intended. You should use this tool in the same way.

One last point: In all the examples used here, single words made up the list. As mentioned earlier, however, the linker comma can also be used to connect a series of phrases or clauses.

> 15. When Carla makes dinner for her **family,** she does not cook her dog or her **cat,** she does not cook her frog or her **gnat, and** she does not cook her hog or her bat.

She is, it turns out, a vegetarian. She makes cheese enchiladas.

Correct the **first sentence** in each example below. Extra spacing should give you room to write directly on this page. If the first sentence is correct as written, however, place a letter C next to it. Suggested answers follow.

1. The author of *Mindset: The New Psychology of Success* is a psychologist Carol S. Dweck.[26]

2. She taught at Columbia University Harvard University and the University of Illinois before joining the faculty at Stanford University in 2004.

3. Professor Dweck argues that individuals place themselves on a continuum depending on their view of where their abilities come from.

4. She describes this self-assessment as implicit which means individuals are unaware of it.

5. Everyone has abilities in areas like intelligence creativity and talent.

6. Some people believe their success reflects innate ability a fixed theory of intelligence. This orientation indicates a "fixed mindset." People with such feelings about themselves believe there is little they can do to change.

7. Such persons strive to look smart all the time fearing that others will think they are dumb.

8. Other individuals believe their success stems from hard work learning and training. This orientation indicates a "growth mindset."

9. Such individuals know they can develop their intelligence creativity and talent.

10. These types of people worry less about making mistakes since learning comes from failure.

11. They are more likely to keep working hard even when faced with a setback.

12. These different mindsets play vital roles affecting every aspect of people's lives.

13. Professor Dweck asserts that those possessing a growth mindset live less stressful more successful and happier lives.

---

[26] Carol S. Dweck, *Mindset: The New Psychology of Success* (New York: Random House, 2006). Since my summary only scratches the surface of her argument, I recommend you read the book. She has kindly made a pdf version available using a search engine.

The word or phrase in **boldface** shows the suggested placement of the linker comma. In some cases, use of the linker comma may be optional, depending on the flow you wish to establish.

1. The author of *Mindset: The New Psychology of Success* is a **psychologist,** Carol S. Dweck.

2. She taught at Columbia **University,** Harvard **University,** and the University of **Illinois,** before joining the faculty at Stanford University in 2004.

3. Professor Dweck argues that individuals place themselves on a **continuum,** depending on their view of where their abilities come from.

4. She describes this self-assessment as **implicit,** which means individuals are unaware of it.

5. Everyone has abilities in areas like **intelligence, creativity,** and talent.

6. Some people believe their success reflects innate **ability,** a fixed theory of intelligence. This orientation indicates a "fixed mindset." People with such feelings about themselves believe there is little they can do to change.

7. Such persons strive to look smart all the **time,** fearing that others will think they are dumb.

8. Other individuals believe their success stems from hard **work, learning,** and training. This orientation indicates a "growth mindset."

9. Such individuals know they can develop their **intelligence, creativity,** and talent.

10. These types of people worry less about making **mistakes,** since learning comes from failure.

11. They are more likely to keep working **hard,** even when faced with a setback.

12. These different mindsets play vital **roles,** affecting every aspect of people's lives.

13. Professor Dweck asserts that those possessing a growth mindset live less **stressful,** more **successful,** and happier lives.

Comment: All of these sentences are hard to punctuate, especially #2. It features both a list and an afterthought, which can be difficult to sort out. As mentioned in the text, when a list of three occurs, I recommend placing a comma in front of *and,* the American way. But what do you think?

Exercise: Write 3-4 sentences about your own or your best friend's mindset using a linker comma in each. As always, these punctuation recommendations might differ when the sentences are combined into two or more paragraphs. Where would you make the divisions and why? How would your punctuation decisions change? I have placed my suggestions for paragraph divisions in the footnote below.[27]

My or My Best Friend's Mindset, using a linker comma in each sentence.

---

[27] I would probably like three paragraphs, with the divisions coming after #2 and #7.

Correct the **first sentence** in each example below. Extra spacing should give you room to write directly on this page. If the first sentence is correct as written, however, place a letter C next to it. Suggested answers follow.

1. Many observers have thought about how people can move from a fixed to a growth mindset.

2. Among them is a photographer Andrew S. Gibson. He suggests that people with growth mindsets display certain characteristics.[28]

3. Curiosity drives successful people who constantly ask questions. What happens if I do that? How does this work?

4. High achieving individuals do not fear failure but embrace it.

5. Those with a growth mindset understand that there are no shortcuts only hard work and learning produce success.

6. Successful people love what they do which makes the effort enjoyable.

7. A growth mindset requires a desire to learn new skills new ideas and sometimes new values. It also demands the discipline to find time to study.

8. People who succeed display a positive attitude toward life not a negative one. Working hard is difficult when you see everything around you in negative terms.

9. Successful people act rather than waiting for something to happen.

10. Action requires that people set goals which must be realistic measurable and time specific. For example, I want to publish a photograph in a magazine by the end of the year.

11. Successful individuals get to know people who can help them achieve their goals which gurus call networking. A guru is a teacher.

12. No one said success is easy only that you'll lead a better happier and healthier life as a result.

---

[28] Andrew S. Gibson, *The Creative Photographer* (ebook: The Creative Photographer Store, 2017). If you are interested in learning photography, check out Mr. Gibson's blog for his other ebooks: andrew@creative-photographer.com.

The word or phrase in **boldface** shows the suggested placement of the linker comma. In some cases, its use may be optional, depending on the flow you wish to establish.

1. Many observers have thought about how people can move from a fixed to a growth mindset.

2. Among them is a **photographer,** Andrew S. Gibson. He suggests that people with growth mindsets display certain characteristics.

3. Curiosity drives successful **people,** who constantly ask questions. What happens if I do that? How does this work?

4. High achieving individuals do not fear **failure,** but embrace it.

5. Those with a growth mindset understand that there are no short**cuts,** only hard work and learning produce success.

6. Successful people love what they **do,** which makes the effort enjoyable.

7. A growth mindset requires a desire to learn new **skills, new ideas, and sometimes new values.** It also demands the discipline to find time to study.

8. People who succeed display a positive attitude toward **life,** not a negative one. Working hard is difficult when you see everything around you in negative terms.

9. Successful people **act,** rather than waiting for something to happen.

10. Action requires that people set **goals, which must be realistic, measurable, and time specific.** For example, I want to publish a photograph in a magazine by the end of the year.

11. Successful individuals get to know people who can help them achieve their **goals,** which gurus call networking. A guru is a teacher.

12. No one said success is **easy, only that you'll lead a better, happier, and healthier life** as a result.

Comment: Number 1 seems correct, at least to me. Most of the rest probably need a linker comma. Probably. But what about #4 and #9? In both cases, you could eliminate the pause and the sentence would read smoothly. What do you think? Would you use the linker comma or not?

Exercise: Write 3-4 sentences about your own mindset, using a linker comma in each. Discuss how you could change to increase your chances of long-term success.

As always, these recommendations for using the linker comma might differ when the sentences are combined into two or more paragraphs. Where would you make the divisions and why? How would your punctuation decisions change in a paragraph context?

The sentences in this worksheet could be divided into three paragraphs, after #2 and perhaps after #8. As with the previous worksheet, the latter division is arbitrary, designed to avoid a too long paragraph. If you constructed the essay in this manner, would your punctuation decisions change?

My Own Mindset and How I Could Change to Increase My Chances for Long-term Success

5. Looking beyond the Comma to More Marvels of Punctuation.

Your punctuation toolbox contains four types of comma: the introducer, joiner, inserters, and linker. Along with the three full-stops, these tools allow you to construct sentences and paragraphs as you would a house: carefully, precisely, and beautifully. Like a builder, you control your writing style. You're using tools, not obeying rules.

Just as builders begin a job by gathering the appropriate tools, a **tool-based approach** to punctuation places you in charge. Even as a beginner, however, you may want to add more tools to your toolbox, such as the colon and semicolon.

These marks allow you to vary the length of the pause in creative and interesting ways. But how can you do this so that readers become engaged rather than confused? After all, the sentences that result may become longer and more complex. Sometimes the paragraphs will, too. You will have more decisions to make. You will also have more control over what you say, how you say it, and what you mean.

That's fun. It's like developing a new superpower. It increases your ability to engage and influence people with your writing.

Your Notes Here

_____

_____

_____

_____

_____

_____

_____

VII. Colon

Recall that a period marks the end of a sentence containing both a subject and verb.
It says stop, this thought is complete. Colons also appear at the end of a sentence. Those
vertical dots (:), however, mean something entirely different. If a period is like a stop-light, a
colon is like a green-light. It says: Go on through the intersection, more information follows.

Your punctuation toolbox contains two types of colons, each with a different function. The
first serves a grammatical purpose, which means it provides a tool for your creativity. The
second organizes items that cannot be dealt with in other ways. In this case, alas, you should
learn the rules for their use.

1. Forward-looking Colon

A **forward-looking colon introduces information that adds detail or explains the
sentence or phrase preceding it.** It functions as a "**mark of expectation**" at the end of a
sentence.[29] When used effectively, this tool tells you to anticipate, perhaps with pleasure,
what comes next. The impact can create emphasis that makes readers interested in what you
might say. As you will see, this effect is often enhanced by the combining the forward-looking
colon with the comma.

> 1. Ronald read three books this summer.

Although this sentence is grammatically correct, it leaves readers unsatisfied. What books? A
list of the books Ronald read would be helpful to readers, stimulating curiosity.

> 2. Ronald read three books this **summer.** He read *The Very Hungry Caterpillar, The
>   Giver,* and *The House of the Scorpion.*

This version improves on the first because it provides the missing information. But,
depending on your purpose, the period, with its full-stop, may create an awkward pace. A
forward-looking colon rescues the situation, grabbing readers' attention.

> 3. Ronald read three books this **summer:** *The Very Hungry Caterpillar, The Giver,* and
>   *The House of the Scorpion.*

In #3, the forward-looking colon invites readers to go on through the intersection, to look for

---

[29] The phrase is Harry Shaw's, p. 60.

the new information. Notice that the normal rules of capitalization apply with the forward-looking colon. For example, proper nouns should be capitalized and common nouns should not. In example #3, *The Very Hungry Caterpillar* is the title of a book. The first letter of the title, *The,* should be capitalized.

> 4. In each of these books, the author creates an interesting **character:** Fred, Jonas, and Matteo.

This example could have been written using a period. *In each of these books, the author creates an interesting* **character.** *Their names are Fred, Jonas, and Matteo.* Although this strategy works, it slows the reader down. The forward-looking colon makes example #4 shorter, punchier, and more thought-provoking.

Some writers employ the forward-looking colon along with a rhetorical fragment. It produces a forceful, interest-creating effect. But make sure it looks intentional.

> 5. Which of these characters must eat to find his destiny? Only **one: Fred**.

> 6. Fred stuffed himself with the following **items:** a pickle, a piece of sausage, and a lollipop. They cover all the food groups.

Once again, even though the clause in front of the colon in #6 constitutes a sentence and could be ended with a period, it leaves the reader hanging. What items? Inserting a period provides one solution: *Only Fred ate the following* **items.** *He ate a pickle, a piece of sausage, and a lollipop.* If, however, you want to avoid repetition and make readers attend to your point, the forward-looking colon may provide a better tool.

> 7. Of course, Fred differs from the **others: He** is a caterpillar.

The punchline following the forward-looking colon in #7 creates interest, especially if you haven't read the book. So pull this item out of your toolbox and use it. Your readers will enjoy it and they will look forward to what you have to say.

Notice that #7 differs from the previous examples: The forward-looking colon points toward a new sentence. Grammarians differ about whether to capitalize the first word in such instances. I always **capitalize:** *He* *is a caterpillar.* Although I suggest you do as well, this is not a rule you should worry about. Choose either style, just be consistent.

Another example shows how to generate curiosity with a forward-looking colon:

> 8. The drug lord in *The House of Scorpion,* El Patrón, cared only about two **things.** He cared about wealth and power.

9. The drug lord in *The House of Scorpion,* El Patrón, cared only about two **things:** wealth and power.

Both examples convey the same information. Inserting the forward-looking colon in #9, however, produces more impact on readers. Good writers create interest with a simple and forceful writing style. Punctuation tools, such as the forward-looking colon, help achieve this goal.

As these examples show, the forward-looking colon stimulates interest, adds clarity, and creates an effective pace. But observe the pattern in each example: The last word before the colon is a noun. *Ronald read three books this summer: The Giver, The House of the Scorpion, and The Very Hungry Caterpillar.* The noun is *summer.* Go back and look at the other examples and you will see the same thing.

Grammarians argue that this pattern, a noun before the colon, is correct. They claim further that it is wrong to precede the colon with a verb.[30] That's right. Wrong. It's the rule. For example, they would call this construction incorrect: *The books Ronald read this summer* **are:** *The Giver, The House of the Scorpion, and The Very Hungry Caterpillar.* They would point out that you have what seems to be a better alternative: the linker comma. *The books Ronald read this summer* **are The** *Giver, The House of the Scorpion, and The Very Hungry Caterpillar.* Although this sentence is grammatically correct, it is also boring.

I don't like boring. And neither do readers. Your teachers will probably agree with the grammar police and mark you down for placing a colon after *are:* or any other verb. As in the previous sentence. But if, for some reason, you want the added punch provided by the colon, go for it. Just be prepared to defend yourself. Remind your teachers that **tools are better than rules**. Ask them if they have read anything by Kurt Vonnegut. You'll see why in the next section.

Rules, smules. Right? But now we turn to two special contexts. In both cases, you should learn the rules. What can I say? It happens.

2. Spacer Colon

The **spacer colon serves a unique purpose: as a placeholder separating items**. Even as a placeholder, however, the spacer colon suggests expectation, that something follows. As you will see below: First come hours, then minutes. Okay, but how do writers separate the two on the page or screen? You can write the flight took two hours, thirty minutes, which is plain enough. But how do you write the same thing using numbers? With a period: 2.30? A comma: 2,30? A semicolon: 2;30? Perhaps a colon: 2:30?

As David Crystal describes it in his history of punctuation, over the centuries all these marks have been used.[31] Eventually, however, a consensus emerged: Use the colon as a spacer. You can, of course, defy this agreement. You always have a choice in life, even if it's just to

---

[30] See William Strunk and E. B. White, p. 8; Harry Shaw, p. 63.
[31] David Crystal, pp. 31-45, 216-26.

say no. To deny choice is to escape from freedom, to escape from your essential humanity. But what would be the point of using a different mark? Employing the spacer colon in the ways described below provides a convenient way to communicate clearly. In this case, I recommend that you learn and follow the rules.

Even given your decision to follow the rules, there remain inconsistencies in how to read both the spacer colon and the units it separates. Sometimes you treat the spacer colon like a comma or a period when reading it, while other times you ignore it as if it's not there. In addition, you sometimes do not read the units separated by spacer colon literally. Rather, you either silently insert the additional words left out or say them aloud.

1. The next meeting of the Captain Underpants Fan Club will take place on Wednesday night at 7:30 p.m.

2. It took me only 2:30 to read the latest Captain Underpants book.

Use a spacer colon to separate hours and minutes. Examples #1 and #2 show this rule. They also illustrate the different ways of reading the spacer colon with units of time.

Read #1 out loud and you will be understood. The meeting is *Wednesday night at seven-thirty p.m.* There is no pause for the spacer colon. It's as if it did not exist.

But if you read #2 out loud, without the colon, listeners might not understand you. Try it: *It took me only two-thirty to read the latest Captain Underpants book.* The phrasing sounds odd. Rather, you would normally say *It took me only 2 hours, 30 minutes to read the latest Captain Underpants book.* To which your best friend would reply: Why so long? But I digress from the topic.

In example #2, you supply (silently if you are reading) the implied words *hours* and *minutes.* In this and other uses, the spacer colon often acts like a comma. A small pause occurs as it is read.

3. Jesus tells the parable of the Good Samaritan in Luke 10:25-37.

Use a spacer colon to cite chapters and verse in the Bible. Theologians and others familiar with the Bible might read this sentence as written. They would understand each other. For the rest of us, however, it would be perfectly acceptable to read the sentence (possibly silently) as *Jesus tells the parable of the Good Samaritan in Luke, Chapter 10, Verses 25 to 37.* You add the implied words. Again, the colon signifies a slight pause, like a comma.

4. After we ate the alligator stew, the ratio of barf jokes to fart jokes was 3:1.

Use a spacer colon when writing ratios. A ratio tells how much of one thing compares to another. Read this example saying *to* where the colon appears and without a pause: *At the party last night, the ratio of barf to fart jokes was 3 to1.* Once again, you read it as if the colon wasn't there.

5. Leonard Beeghley wrote a book titled *Homicide: A Sociological Explanation.*[32]

Use a spacer colon to distinguish between the title and subtitle of a book. You don't read the spacer colon in this example. Rather, you treat it like a comma and pause slightly.

6. Dear Mr. Velazquez:

Insert a spacer colon in the salutation of a formal letter. A salutation is the greeting in a message. Use of the last name indicates that this is a formal letter or message. The colon functions like a period, requiring a full stop when reading it. By the way, in an informal letter, signified by a first name in the salutation, use a comma: *Dear **Tony**,*. In both cases, the colon and the comma serve as silent spacers to provide a transition to the body of the letter.

The spacer colon functions like a good filing system. It keeps certain aspects of a sentence organized by separating hours from minutes, chapters from verses, books titles from subtitles, and the salutation from the body of a letter. For this reason, using these rules requires no judgment. Simply learn and remember them. Sorry.

But we're not done with following the rules. You may have noticed earlier that I referred to the author of *A Wrinkle in Time* as **Ms.** L'Engle and mentioned in example #1 on p. 66 that the meeting will take place at 7:30 **p.m.** These examples show that periods have spacer functions, too. And so do commas.

3. Spacer Period and Comma

Like the spacer colon, spacer periods and spacer commas function as placeholders separating items. They also serve as organizational tools that everyone uses. And, as before, you have a choice about whether to follow the consensus. But what would be the point of inserting some other mark? I suggest you follow the rules. Once again, how you read or say the result varies, which you can figure out. Just say the examples out loud.

Use a spacer period as a decimal point. The paperback version of *A Wrinkle in Time* costs $7.23. Your temperature is 98.6 degrees. Here and below, the period remains a small dot with a big impact.

Use a spacer period in email and internet addresses. My email address is leonardbeeghley@gmail.com. A useful website for learning grammar and punctuation is the Purdue Online Writing Lab, which can be found at: https://owl.english.purdue.edu/owl/. That's the official address. Using your search engine, just type "Purdue owl" and you'll get there.

Use a spacer period with certain abbreviations. Examples are Mr. for Mister, Jan. for January, St. for street, lb. for pound, Dr. for doctor, and a.m. and p.m. for the time of day.

---

[32] Leonard Beeghley, *Homicide: A Sociological Explanation* (New York: Roman & Littlefield, 2008). Note also the colon within the parentheses that separates the city of publication and the name of the publisher. Handle it as a comma.

By the way, a.m. and p.m. reflect the division of the twenty-four-hour day into two twelve-hour segments. The abbreviations come from the Latin phrases "ante meridiem" and "post meridiem." They mean, respectively, "before noon" and "after noon." Just so you know.

Use a spacer comma to close a letter. At the end of a letter, I might conclude with Best wishes, Leonard. Or, more informally: Cheers, Leonard. You do not place a period after the closing name.

Use a spacer comma to separate thousands and millions. For example, you would write 1,000 for one thousand and 1,000,000 for one million. The consensus about using the spacer comma in this way only applies to the U.S. Other nations use a spacer period to separate thousands and millions.

There are probably other examples of the spacer period and spacer comma. Can you think of any?

Your Notes Here

_____

_____

_____

_____

_____

_____

_____

_____

_____

Correct **all the sentences** in each example below, **using forward-looking colons, spacer colons, spacer periods, and commas where necessary. When inserting a forward-looking colon, capitalize the following word if appropriate.** If the first sentence seems correct as written, however, place a letter C next to it. Suggested answers follow.

1. Dear Dr Mejia

2. It is now 330 am and I worried about my appointment next Friday Feb 2.

3. My flight from Chicago to Durham that morning only takes 245.

4. It arrives at 1150 am That should give me plenty of time to get to your office.

5. I know that you are going to perform three tasks filling the cavity on my canine tooth pulling the upper left wisdom tooth and placing a cap on my front incisor.

6. I gnawed on my fingernails for the last hour before realizing what was bothering me what are fingernails made of?

7. My granddaughter Belle once made an astute remark you have a teacher. Her name is Google.

8. With Belle in mind I turned on my computer and logged onto Wikipedia.

9. After typing in my question the answer appeared fingernails are composed of a protein called alpha-keratin.

10. Scientists also found that alpha-keratin constitutes the main substance in various animal parts hooves horns and hair. The last is a real surprise.

11. Of course humans don't have either hooves or horns but they do have hair.

12. Hair is like a fingernail it is easy to cut.

13. Hair is like a fingernail in another way it doesn't hurt when you cut it.

14. Now in the middle of the night we have arrived at an important philosophical question why do teeth hurt when you drill into them but hair does not when you cut it? After all they are made of the same substance.

15. In addition one other question occurred to me do you think these three tasks are too much to accomplish in one hour?

16. In the meantime I will find comfort in the Bible especially Psalm 234.

17. Yours Sincerely Leonard Beeghley

The word or phrase in **boldface** shows the suggested placement of the forward-looking colon, spacer colon, spacer period, and commas. In some cases, use of the forward-looking colon or comma may be optional, depending on the flow you wish to establish.

1. Dear **Dr. Mejia:**

2. It is now **3:30 a.m.** and I worried about my appointment next **Friday, Feb.** 2.

3. My flight from Chicago to Durham that morning only takes **2:45**.

4. It arrives at **11:50 a.m**. That should give me plenty of time to get to your office.

5. I know that you are going to perform three **tasks: filling** the cavity on my canine **tooth,** pulling the upper left wisdom **tooth,** and placing a cap on my front incisor.

6. I gnawed on my fingernails for the last hour before realizing what was bothering **me: What** are fingernails made of?

7. My **granddaughter, Belle,** once made an astute **remark: You** have a teacher. Her name is Google.

8. With Belle in **mind,** I turned on my computer and logged onto Wikipedia.

9. After typing in my **question,** the answer **appeared: Fingernails** are composed of a protein called alpha-keratin.

10. Scientists also found that alpha-keratin constitutes the main substance in various animal **parts: hooves, horns,** and hair. The last is a real surprise.

11. **Of course,** humans don't have either hooves or **horns: But** they do have hair.

12 Hair is like a **fingernail: It** is easy to cut.

13. Hair is like a fingernail in another **way: It** doesn't hurt when you cut it.

14. **Now,** in the middle of the **night,** we have arrived at an important philosophical **question: Why** do teeth hurt when you drill into them but hair does not when you cut it? After **all,** they are made of the same substance.

15. In **addition,** one other question occurred to **me: Do** you think these three tasks are too much to accomplish in one hour?

16. In the **meantime,** I will find comfort in the **Bible:** especially **Psalm 23:4.**

17. Yours **Sincerely,** Leonard Beeghley

Comment: In this worksheet, spacer colons and spacer periods are necessary in #1, 2, 3, 4, and 16. A spacer comma appears in #17. You must simply remember to use them.

The remaining items require your judgment. For example, in #7 you might create a compound sentence after the forward-looking colon: *You have a **teacher, h**er name is Google.* If you see the sentence as part of a paragraph, this change might improve the rhythm.

Before continuing, let's consider sentences #9-13 in the worksheet. Each shows how to use the forward-looking colon in a grammatically correct way. That is, of course, the point of the lesson. But what happens when they are placed together in a paragraph? I've reprinted the sentences as written below, but without the numbers attached to them. Please read what is now a paragraph out loud.

> After typing in my question, the answer appeared: Fingernails are composed of a protein called alpha-keratin. Scientists also found that alpha-keratin constitutes the main substance in various animal parts: hooves, horns, and hair. This last is a real surprise. Of course, humans don't have either hooves or horns: But they do have hair. Hair is like a fingernail: It is easy to cut. Hair is like a fingernail in another way: It doesn't hurt when cut.

I hope you noticed the choppiness, mainly due to all the colons. The rhythm, or lack thereof, makes for difficult reading. This example shows why **punctuation decisions must be made in the context of the paragraph in which the sentence appears.**

Rewriting the material, as shown below, produces a paragraph that sticks together and is easier to read. This exercise anticipates the next section, which discusses the importance of paragraph construction and rewriting. I placed the changes in bold.

> After typing in the question, **I found the answer**. Fingernails are composed of a protein called alpha-keratin. Scientists **say that it also constitutes the main** substance in various animal parts: hooves, horns, and hair. This last is a real surprise. Of course, humans don't have either hooves or **horns.** But they do have hair. **Moreover,** hair is like a fingernail **in that** it is easy to **cut. It also** doesn't hurt when cut.

The revision includes only one colon. The new paragraph also mixes longer and shorter sentences in order to make reading easier and more enjoyable. I will come back to these issues.

One last point: Look at #16. Although I used a forward-looking colon after *Bible:*, a linker comma would work just as well. Tools provide you with choices. Use them.

One final last point, also in #16: In *Psalm 23:4*, which you would read as *chapter 23, verse 4,* the psalmist writes "Yea, though I walk through the valley of the shadow of death, I will fear no evil; for You are with me; Your rod and Your staff, they comfort me." This translation is from the King James version. The wording varies with more recent translations.

Exercise: Write a paragraph of 3-4 sentences about your worst experience with a doctor or dentist. Use both types of colons and commas where appropriate.

My Worst Experience
with a Doctor
or Dentist

VIII.
Semicolon

This little dot goes right here.

A period ends a sentence. All forms of the comma appear in the middle of a sentence. The semicolon (;) looks like "a period balanced on top of a comma."[33] This appearance implies that it exists between the two, which is accurate. On the one hand, the semicolon speeds up the flow of a sentence by avoiding a full stop. On the other hand, it suggests the need for a pause, albeit a slightly longer one than provided by the comma.

Your punctuation toolbox contains two types of semicolons: the connector semicolon and managing semicolon. Before describing their purposes, however, I want to introduce you to Kurt Vonnegut, a 20th century American novelist. Mr. Vonnegut wrote satire. Satire is a style of writing in which authors use sarcasm, scorn, and humor to expose absurdity. Mr. Vonnegut directed special contempt at two-faced politicians and other public figures in the United States. He used satire to express certain values: People should treat one another with respect and government should protect ordinary citizens from exploitation by the rich and powerful.

In making these arguments, Mr. Vonnegut wrote simply, without adornment. He opened one of his last books with what he called the most important rule of writing: "Do not use semicolons." Their only purpose, he said, is for writers to show off.[34] He hated pretension, trying to impress others, whether in writing or in daily life. To prove his point about the semicolon, he proposed to write the entire book without using this tool even once. This is satire, so perhaps he was kidding.

He wasn't. In showing off their skills some authors display an unfortunate case of semicolonitis: Those afflicted with this disease use the mark over and over again. Only writers who are full of themselves contract this illness. Kurt Vonnegut proposed to illustrate his argument by showing that writers can get along perfectly well without this tool.

But is he correct? Can you, as a beginner, get along without the semicolon? Yes. But **tools are better than rules,** even Kurt Vonnegut's rule. The trick is to use punctuation tools effectively, without pretension. In deciding whether to link two clauses with a semicolon, consider what is going on in the paragraph as a whole.

---

[33] The phrase comes from Richard Lederer and John Shore, *Comma Sense: A Fundamental Guide to Punctuation* (New York: St. Martin's Press, 2005), p. 43.

[34] Kurt Vonnegut, *A Man Without a Country: A Memoir of Life in George Bush's America* (New York: Seven Stories Press, 2005), p. 23. One can only imagine how Mr. Vonnegut would view today's political scene.

1. Connector Semicolon

The **connector semicolon joins two ideas in one sentence; each is an independent clause**. You may recall that an **independent clause** can stand alone as a sentence because it contains both a subject and verb.

When the connector semicolon attaches independent clauses, it functions like a bridge connecting landmasses separated by water. But, as Kurt Vonnegut suggested, not every river need a bridge over it. There are other choices, such as boats or tunnels. You might also want to avoid crossing it at all. Perhaps the barrier formed by the river is useful.

In writing, you should ask whether the connector semicolon provides a useful bridge. After all, you now possess several other punctuation tools. Why use a connector semicolon instead of either a joiner comma or the simple word "and"? Why not select a period? These are the questions Mr. Vonnegut was raising and you should consider.

When they are not showing off, **writers use a connector semicolon for two reasons.** First, they want to emphasize a special relationship between the clauses. Second, they want to maintain a positive rhythm for readers. Both of these conditions rarely occur and so does the connector semicolon. Look back at the pages of this book and observe how few times this mark appears.

> 1. The Principal, Mr. Krupp, bullied George and **Harold; later,** they turned him into Captain Underpants.

These two clauses read perfectly well as separate sentences: *The Principal, Mr. Krupp, bullied George and* **Harold. Later,** *they turned him into Captain Underpants.* Given their close relationship, however, inserting a connector semicolon might be effective. I placed a transitional word and an introducer comma after the semicolon *Harold; later,* to provide for a smooth read. The result is not too long, only 15 words. The context, which is to say the paragraph, would determine the usefulness of this tool. Perhaps you wrote a series of short sentences before and after. In that situation, connecting the clauses in #1 with a connector semicolon would break the sentence pattern and make reading easier.

> 2. Don't ask how they did **it;** it's a long story.

Example #2 does not need a transitional term after the connector semicolon. Again, these two clauses can stand separately. *Don't ask how they did* **it.** *It's a long story.* When combined with the connector semicolon, however, the cadence displays a catchy rhythm that gets the reader's attention. We'll come back to the adventures of George and Harold in the last worksheet.

In the meantime, maybe Kurt Vonnegut's "rule" functions best as a caution: Don't use any punctuation tool just to show off. When should you use the semicolon? What about the colon? And who cares about the comma? All the marks reviewed so far provide potential answers. Sometimes all of them will be grammatically correct. **Which tool you choose ought** to reflect the tempo you want to establish, the meaning you want to convey, and the context in which it appears.

> 3. Abe loves to wash and comb his hairy knuckles. Luis needs to barf.

Creating two sentences separated by a period implies there is no connection between Abe and Luis. Maybe they happened to enter the bathroom at the same time: Abe to wash and comb his hairy knuckles, and Luis with an upset stomach. If so, you will probably need another sentence or two to explain the situation. If, however, a connection does exist, then you might want to avoid the full stop and use one of the other marks.

> 4. Abe loves to wash and comb his hairy knuckles, and Luis needs to barf.

Oh, oh. Perhaps Luis reacts with such disgust to Abe's luxurious and beautiful knuckle hair that he must vomit. In this example, the connecting word *and* preceded by a joiner comma suggests the linkage in a simple, easy to read way.

> 5. Abe loves to wash and comb his hairy knuckles; as a result, Luis needs to barf.

In #5, the connector semicolon does more than suggest a linkage. It provides a bridge to the next clause. Inserting the transitional phrase *as a result*, makes the causal relationship explicit. This example also provides a good reading experience.

> 6. Abe loves to wash and comb his hairy knuckles: Luis needs to barf.

The forward-looking colon drives the point home: Abe's revolting actions cause Luis's intestinal trouble. Again, readers will have no trouble with this format.

As a writer, you strive to explain your meaning clearly and effectively. Examples #3-6 all read smoothly. Each, however, alters the meaning of the sentence in a somewhat different way. Which tool should you choose? We come back again to the matter of judgment.

Given this subject matter, #6 might work best. The forward-looking colon emphasizes Luis's reaction. If his distress was due to something less gross than hairy knuckles, the joiner comma in #4 might be more appropriate. Although the connector semicolon in #5 would usually be my last choice, selecting it would not be showing off. Rather, the context would determine the decision.

Kurt Vonnegut also emphasized the importance of context. He kept his word and used no semicolons in the entire book: until near the end. He writes that people with imagination "can look into someone's face and see stories **there;** to everyone else, a face will just be a face." He then observes that "I've just used a semicolon, which at the outset I told you never to use. It is to make a point that I did it. The point is: Rules only take us so far, even good rules."[35]

---

[35] Vonnegut, p. 134. The boldface is mine.

"Rules only take us so far, even good rules." This statement provides a good principle for organizing your life. **With regard to punctuation, your decisions should reflect your judgment in light of what is going on.**

Finally, as a sidebar, I hope you noticed Mr. Vonnegut's last line. He wrote *The point **is:** Rules only take us so far, even good rules.* Oh, oh. The grammar police won't like the colon following the verb. Tell them to read the sentence, rather than worry about the rule. Is it effective? Does it drive his point home? **Tools are better than rules.**

2. Managing Semicolon

On rare occasions, a long sentence becomes so full of commas that readers find it difficult to follow. Remember: It's easy for them to quit. In this context, **a writer might insert a managing semicolon to substitute for one or more of the commas.** This tool functions to keep a sentence organized so readers can keep track of the argument. The managing semicolon marks a special place for them to pause a little and catch their breath. It's like inserting a half note after a quarter note.

> 1. "Lord, make me an instrument of your peace. Where there is **hatred,** let me sow **love;** where there is **injury, pardon;** where there is **doubt, faith;** where there is **despair, hope;** where there is **darkness, light;** and where there is **sadness, joy.**"[36]

The famous "Peace Prayer," falsely attributed to Saint Francis, provides a vivid example of how managing semicolons can keep a sentence organized. After the short introduction, the anonymous writer establishes a repetitive rhythm in the 34-word second sentence by using introducer commas and managing semicolons. The introducer comma asks the reader to pause briefly, the managing semicolon suggests a slightly longer pause. Without both marks, this passage would be difficult reading; with them, it becomes a thing of beauty. Moreover, although it is a complex paragraph, it reads so smoothly that it looks easy to write.

It's not. Few of us have this level of skill. Most of the time, as a beginner, you will only create trouble for yourself if you try to write a long sentence like this. Instead, do the hard work. Rewrite your sentence so that it becomes shorter and does not require so many commas and other marks. Remember: A grammatically correct short sentence is better than a mistake-filled long sentence.

The next section focuses on rewriting a long sentence so that its meaning becomes clear and its impact greater. This process illustrates how to improve your writing skills. You begin with a first try, a draft of what you want to say. It's unclear or reads poorly. So you think about it. You insert new words, take words out, or alter punctuation tools. Each change leads you to reassess what you've written. As you will see, colons and semicolons are now part of that process.

---

[36] No one seems to know who wrote this prayer, except that it certainly wasn't Saint Francis. To learn more, look for "Peace Prayer of St. Francis" with your search engine.

Let's Eat Grandma? © 2018 Leonard Beeghley

IX. Using Punctuation Tools to Improve Your Writing Skills

By shifting the emphasis to tools from rules, a **tool-based approach** to punctuation and improving your writing skills places you in control. It encourages you to choose the most effective way to convey your message. So how does a tool-based approach work in practice?

The answer requires remembering that sentences do not stand alone; they exist in a context. That context is the paragraph. In emphasizing that punctuation decisions should always reflect what is going on, I refer to the paragraph.

Recall that a **paragraph** usually consists of several sentences dealing with a single topic. The traditional paragraph you're taught to write constitutes a short essay that displays a beginning, middle, and end. Brenda's paragraph, in which she explained how she became friends with Jamelle, provided one example. The revised paragraphs following Worksheets #1 and #9 provided others.[37]

In a traditional paragraph that produces its intended effect, the sentences fit together like notes in a piece of music. Each advances the argument. When you read them, their tempo increases or slows down as the writer intends. A stable rhythm within and between sentences makes readers want to continue; a poor one makes them want to quit.

The examples in this section show how you can engage readers and make them interested in what you have to say. The trick is to analyze what you have written and rewrite it to make your point clear. The word analysis means to inspect the parts of something to learn what they do and how they fit together. You might, for example, study the parts of a house, the parts of a mathematical formula, or the parts of a chemical substance. In our case, we are going to examine the parts of a paragraph.

We are going to look at how the words, phrases, and sentences fit, or don't fit, together. And how they can be improved to form a well-organized argument. We are also going to look at how changes in punctuation affect rhythm and meaning.

---

[37] You should learn more about the logic of paragraph construction. See Roy Peter Clark, pp. 93-97, and Sheridan Baker, pp. 41-58. My friends Strunk and White argue that you should "make the paragraph the unit of composition." I agree; see pp. 15-17.

To see how this process works, I suggest you go slowly. Remember, the goal is to push the discussion forward in a way that grabs and holds the attention of readers.

Before proceeding, here are two rewriting skills you should learn. Both will be illustrated in the analysis below. First, when you consider what's on the page, you must be willing to say goodbye to the ones you love: those wonderful words, phrases, and punctuation marks that don't fit. Once you learn to recognize which loved-ones fail to advance the argument and cast them away, your writing will improve. Second, read what you have written out loud. You may have noticed how often I suggest doing this. Words on the page have sounds, even if we don't say them. Reading aloud sometimes makes your awkward phrasing clear.

1. In Somalia, where the civil war still rages, western aid workers, in spite of frantic efforts, are unable to operate, and the people, starving, terrified, and desperate, are flooding into neighboring Ethiopia.[38]

Example #1 comprises 33 words and, surprisingly, displays correct punctuation. In addition, the author uses simple words. Only *Ethiopia* is longer than three syllables. Although long sentences can be useful when they present more information in an efficient way, they are wasted if readers become frustrated. That is the problem with #1.

Its eight commas make the sentence too hard to read because the pauses are all the same. It's like playing a song with all quarter notes. There is no rhythm. The effect obscures the argument so that readers must go over it several times. Asking readers to sort through all this chaos 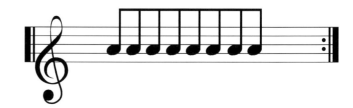 is too much to ask. Despite the importance of the topic, they will quit and go on to something else. To get readers engaged, the passage should be rewritten.

2. In Somalia, where the civil war still rages, western aid workers, in spite of frantic efforts, are unable to **operate;** and the people, starving, terrified, and desperate, are flooding into neighboring Ethiopia.

As the original author points out, inserting a managing semicolon after *operate;* provides a solution. Placing this tool at the most important break organizes the sentence because the slightly extra pause helps readers understand the argument. Try reading it out loud to hear the improvement.

But this solution remains unappealing. Earlier, I described the 34-word "Peace Prayer" as a beautiful piece of writing. In comparison, even with the addition of the managing semicolon, this 33-word sentence lacks impact. This is so especially given the suffering: People are starving. They are terrified. They are desperate. Your task is to get readers involved, to make them as angry about this tragedy as you are.

---

[38] The analysis of this sentence builds on what R. L. Trask begins in *The Penguin Guide to Punctuation* (London: Penguin Books, 1997), pp. 44-45. Examples #1 and #2 are his, which is where he stops. I thought about and rewrote his final version as shown by #3, #4, and #5.

Example #2 does not achieve this goal. Part of the problem is that it still includes seven commas plus the managing semicolon. This is usually too many internal marks for beginners to handle effectively. More importantly, so many commas soften the impact of the message: the starvation, terror, and desperation. In addition, the author uses the linking verb *are* twice, which also dilutes the effect. You want punch, which this sentence does not have.

Consider this version a second draft. As a beginning writer, you should recognize these difficulties, think through what you want to say and how you want to say it, then rewrite. You may need to do this several times.

In the next draft, the bold-face indicates changes and additions, while the strike-outs show deletions. Look carefully at the differences in both punctuation and wording.

3. **Violent civil war still rages i**n Somalia**.**, where the civil war still rages, w **W**estern aid workers **cannot**, in spite of frantic efforts, are unable to operate;**.** **Their efforts are thwarted by the danger. As a result,** and the people, starving, terrified, and desperate, are flooding into neighboring Ethiopia.

In this third draft, I created a paragraph by eliminating the managing semicolon and inserting periods after each independent clause. The longest sentence now comprises only fourteen words. Read it aloud, ignoring the strike-outs. The periods make for a choppy, bullet-like effect, which produces a sense of urgency.

Now look at how I changed the wording: rearranging, omitting, and adding language. The new first sentence states the problem in stark terms: *Violent civil war still rages in Somalia.* Adding *Violent* to the opening sentence makes explicit the source of the *danger*, both to aid workers and citizens. I moved *still* to the front, right before the verb. A violent civil war that *still rages* is extremely destructive and has been going on for a long time. No wonder people are terrified. In this context, *Western aid workers cannot operate. Their efforts are thwarted by the danger.* Thwarted means to prevent or hinder; it provides a strong sound when read aloud. Inserting *As a result,* with its introducer comma, brings the passage to a close.

This short, well-organized paragraph begins with a statement of the problem: the violent civil war that still rages. The middle section explains one impact: Aid workers cannot do their job because of the danger. The paragraph ends with the tragic result: The victims, starving and terrified people, flee into Ethiopia. Most teachers would be satisfied if, as a beginner, you wrote this paragraph. Because each sentence advances the argument, the message is effective.

But you can improve it even more. The three short sentences at the beginning are perhaps too choppy. Also, the fourth sentence still includes a linking verb, *are,* that reduces the force of the argument. Most importantly, however, more is going on than readers are being told. In addition to being terrified, the people are *starving* and readers don't know why. More detail would help. Many beginners make this mistake: They write too little rather than too much. Don't withhold information that readers need and want.

Here again is draft #3, reprinted without marking the changes. Please compare it to draft #4, which follows. Notice the additional information in #4, which helps to clarify the argument.

> Violent civil war still rages in Somalia. Western aid workers cannot operate. Their efforts are thwarted by the danger. As a result, the people, starving, terrified, and desperate, are flooding into neighboring Ethiopia.

In #4, the additions and changes are in bold and deletions crossed out.

> 4. Violent civil war still rages in Somalia. **Militias roam the countryside, destroying crops and killing anyone who opposes them.** Western aid workers cannot **operate;** ~~T~~ their efforts thwarted by the danger. ~~As a result, t~~ The people, starving, terrified, and desperate, ~~are~~ **continue** flooding into neighboring Ethiopia.

In this fourth rewrite, I made no changes to the first sentence. It is short, to the point, and frightening: *Violent civil war still rages in Somalia.*

The middle section now includes two sentences explaining the impact. *Militias roam the countryside, destroying crops and killing anyone who opposes them.* This new sentence provides the missing detail about the source of the starvation. In this dangerous context, *Western aid workers cannot operate; their efforts thwarted by the danger.* Finally, notice that the linking verb, *are,* is gone and I restored the connector semicolon after *operate.*

The concluding sentence of the paragraph now makes perfect sense. I took out *As a result,* because it seemed unnecessary. In place of *are,* I inserted *continue* to emphasize again that the tragedy is ongoing. The active verb adds impact. T*he people, starving, terrified, and desperate,* **continue** *flooding into neighboring Ethiopia.* Here is the final version without marking the changes. Please read it aloud.

> Violent civil war still rages in Somalia. Militias roam the countryside, destroying crops and killing anyone who opposes them. Western aid workers cannot operate; their efforts thwarted by the danger. The people, starving, terrified, and desperate, continue flooding into neighboring Ethiopia.

What do you think? Would you make any more changes? Stop. Be careful. It's a trick question.

It's a trick question because there remains one last problem: that damned semicolon. I made a mistake in restoring it. It was probably to show off. Remember that a semicolon connects two independent clauses. Alas, *their efforts thwarted by the danger* is not a clause; it does not contain both a subject and verb. The phrase is now an afterthought and needs a linker comma. So the paragraph needs a final but important change:

> 5. Violent civil war still rages in Somalia. Militias roam the countryside, destroying crops and killing anyone who opposes them. Western aid workers cannot **operate,** their efforts thwarted by the danger. The people, starving, terrified, and desperate, continue flooding into neighboring Ethiopia.

The original single sentence contained potential. But its lack of rhythm confused readers and made the argument murky. The author's addition of the semicolon in #2 clarified the argument, but its impact remained too soft.

In revisions #3, #4, and #5, I changed the punctuation, inserted and deleted words, and added an explanatory sentence. Eventually, however, the reasoning became easy to understand, and the final result clear, stimulating, and compelling. Reading the revised paragraph should make readers angry, which means you influenced them. And sometimes, not often but sometimes, angry people act.

The process of working on these drafts shows that punctuation tools and writing well go together. They cannot be separated. In that spirit, I present six principles for you, as a beginner, to improve your writing skills.

 First, write and rewrite. Few people compose well-organized arguments the first time they try. It usually takes several drafts to discover your point and then make it clear. This is true for all writers, from beginners to best-selling authors.

 Second, use simple words. You will impress readers more by writing with precision and clarity than by using either big or obscure words. Keep them interested.

 Third, use active verbs as much as possible. Both linking verbs and passive verbs can be effective, as shown by the "Peace Prayer." Active verbs, however, do something. They make your writing more lively, interesting, and persuasive.

 Fourth, avoid too many internal punctuation marks. If a sentence includes more than three or four of these tools, it is probably too long for your skill set. Consider rewriting it.

 Fifth, keep your sentences short, usually less than 20 words. Leave longer sentences to more experienced writers. Even with this maximum length, you should mix longer and shorter sentences to achieve a smooth rhythm.

 Sixth, keep your paragraphs short, usually no more than six to eight sentences. Expert writers will often compose paragraphs longer than this. As a beginner, however, you should learn to make a well-organized argument with this length.

Unfortunately, even if you follow these guidelines and work hard you will not become one of the Beautiful People. Sorry. But, with practice, you will develop into a better writer. That skill will last much longer than superficial popularity. As a result, readers will pay attention to what you have to say. They will also know that you enjoy sharing a meal with your beloved Grandma.

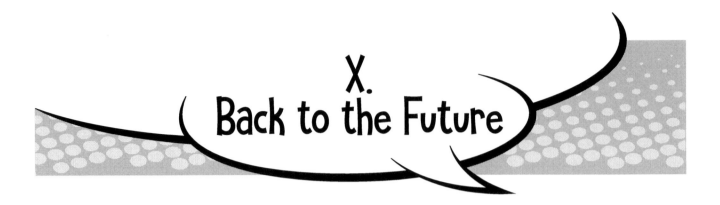

X.
Back to the Future

Alas, your hard work is not finished. You must go back to the future. The phrase comes from the 1985 movie of that title. It's a comedy in which the main character, a teenager named Marty McFly, goes back in time. He meets his future parents when they were teenagers and becomes the love interest of his mother to be. Wait! This outcome can't occur. If Marty's mother marries Marty, then Marty won't be born. The whole idea boggles the mind. So Marty must change the past to fit what happens in the future.

When you think about it, however, the phrase "back to the future" is a little odd. In fact, it's oxymoronic. An oxymoron contradicts itself, like "living dead." Similarly, you cannot literally go back to the future. But the phrase is so suggestive it has entered the language as referring to something from the past being repeated in the present.

No, I don't want you to meet your parents before you were born. That was only funny in the movie, which is worth viewing on one of the cable services. Rather, it's time to return to where this book started.

In addition to being boring, most guides to punctuation teach you to follow rules. They lead you to ask a question like this one: What mark should go here? But this query is misguided. As you have seen, you often have several choices, each of which will be grammatically correct.

A tool-based approach solves this problem. When the marks are treated as tools, you ask a different question: How can I use punctuation to make my message clear, concise, and effective? Good writing does not depend on following rules, it depends on choice. And judgment. Tools are better than rules.

Punctuation provides a set of tools that help you write well. You now have a toolbox consisting of eleven punctuation devices, each with a different function. Taken together, they allow you to control the rhythm and meaning of what you write.

- A **period** ends a sentence, telling readers to stop here.

- A **question mark** ends a sentence by asking readers to reflect on a problem.

- An **exclamation point** ends a sentence with passion and energy.

- An **introducer comma** appears near the beginning of a sentence, telling readers there is more to come.

- A **joiner comma** joins two independent clauses together to form a compound sentence.

- **Inserter commas** tie off a phrase inserted into the middle of a sentence.

- A **linker comma** connects a later part of a sentence to an earlier part.

- A **forward-looking Colon** introduces information that adds detail or explains what preceded it.

- A **spacer colon** functions as a placeholder, separating two items.

- A **connector semicolon** joins two ideas in one sentence; each is an independent clause.

- A **managing semicolon** substitutes for a comma.

Now it is time to assess how much you have learned. Do you understand how to use these tools to end sentences effectively? Do you understand how to regulate the pace of sentences so that your intention is clear? Finally, can you perform these tasks in a larger context: the paragraph? The last worksheet helps you answer these questions.

Punctuate all the sentences in each paragraph in the essay below. You may use all the tools in your toolbox: periods, commas, colons, and semicolons as appropriate. Add capital letters at the beginning of each sentence. Rhetorical fragments may occur, which you may keep or not. You may also rewrite if you can add clarity.

Try not to worry about making mistakes. You can always rewrite your first try. Remember, **tool-based punctuation teaches you that the choice depends on the context.** There are often several ways to compose a grammatically correct sentence, to organize several sentences into an orderly paragraph, and to make them cohere together into a story.

Your job is to use the marks to establish a rhythm that makes each sentence and paragraph flow smoothly from one to another so that the essay engages the reader. In order to make your life interesting, I have omitted capital letters that might indicate the beginning of a sentence. As usual, suggested answers follow.[39]

George and Harold's Revenge

1. Mr. Krupp the school principal hates children especially George and Harold in the first book in the series the kids accidentally discover how to hypnotize Mr. Krupp and turn him into a superhero since superheroes often look like they dress in underwear George and Harold name him Captain Underpants in every book Captain Underpants uses Wedgie Power to defeat his foes only he doesn't know this rather after coming out of the trance he becomes plain old Krupp again mean as ever ready to bully the children

2. no one likes to be bullied *Captain Underpants and the Attack of the Talking Toilets* is the fourteenth book in the series in it the boys' revenge began with a sign on the auditorium door the sign announced The Second Annual Invention Convention the winner of this contest it said would become Principal for the Day George and Harold had only one thought they wanted to win but Mr. Krupp

---

[39] The content of this worksheet is taken loosely from Dav Pilkey's book, cited earlier, *Captain Underpants and the Attack of the Talking Toilets.* I changed the plot slightly to illustrate punctuation. The book is much funnier, as are all fourteen books in the series.

put them in detention to keep them from winning the teachers applauded for they didn't like the children either George and Harold of course snuck out of detention in the auditorium they discovered that Melvin Sneedly had invented the PATSY 2000 an updated copy machine don't ask about the name it is not relevant you need to know however that Melvin's machine does more than copy it transforms pictures into living things what can go wrong

3. to demonstrate his invention Melvin placed a photo of a toilet on PATSY 2000 big mistake after grinding and groaning the machine spit out toilets one after another endlessly their teeth were long their eyeballs glowed blood red they looked fierce angry and hungry worst of all they talked the frightened boys fled the auditorium closed the door and ran into Mr. Krupp

4. instead of listening to the children Mr. Krupp opened the door to the auditorium another big mistake the toilets escaped and ran wild they ate everything they consumed desks teachers and even children everything and everyone was swallowed whole the school became a great big mess Mr. Krupp began to whine after all the carnage he feared losing his job but George and Harold offered him a deal which he accepted they went back to the PATSY 2000 and after searching through magazines placed a photo of a toilet plunger on it after the machine grated and creaked and moaned the Incredible Roboplunger emerged to do battle with the talking toilets

5. the battle cannot be described but it was fierce in the end the Incredible Roboplunger defeated the talking toilets who coughed up everything they had eaten all emerged alive well and scratch free George and Harold got their reward they became Principals for the Day as their first act they put Mr. Krupp and the teachers in detention then they spent the Principal's budget on ice cream and pizza for the kids

The words or phrases in **boldface** show the suggested placement of various punctuation marks. Don't take my suggestions as inherently right. They are not. **Ask yourself what is going on not what Leonard thinks.** Go ahead and make different changes here.

George and Harold's Revenge

1. Mr. **Krupp,** the school **principal,** hates **children,** especially George and **Harold. In** the first book in the **series,** the kids accidentally discover how to hypnotize Mr. Krupp and turn him into a **superhero. Since** superheroes often look like they dress in **underwear,** George and Harold name him Captain **Underpants.** In every **book,** Captain Underpants uses Wedgie Power to defeat his **foes.** Only he doesn't know **this. Rather,** after coming out of the trance he becomes plain old Krupp **again. Mean** as **ever. Ready** to bully the **children.**

   Comment: In this paragraph, the only punctuation tools are periods and commas, which is typical. There are, however, three rhetorical fragments: after *Only, Mean,* and *Ready.* Do you think they are effective? Too many? Instead of a period, one of them could be eliminated by placing a linker comma after "*...defeat his **foes,** only he doesn't know this.*" This would leave only the two rhetorical fragments at the end of the paragraph. What do you think?

2. No one likes to be **bullied.** *Captain Underpants and the Attack of the Talking Toilets* is the fourteenth book in the **series. In it,** the boys' revenge began with a sign on the auditorium **door.** The sign announced The Second Annual Invention **Convention. The** winner of this **contest,** it **said,** would become Principal for the **Day.** George and Harold had only one **thought: T**hey wanted to **win. But** Mr. Krupp put them in detention to keep them from **winning. The** teachers **applauded,** for they didn't like the children **either.** George and **Harold,** of **course,** snuck out of **detention. In** the **auditorium,** they discovered that Melvin Sneedly had invented the PATSY **2000,** an updated copy **machine. Don't** ask about the **name;** it is not **relevant. You** need to **know, however,** that Melvin's machine does more than **copy: It** transforms pictures into living **things.** What can go **wrong?**

   Comment: This paragraph includes two forward-looking colons. In both cases, either periods or semicolons could have been used. It also includes one coordinating semicolon. I could have inserted a period instead. Which tool is most effective?

3. To demonstrate his **invention,** Melvin placed a photo of a toilet on PATSY **2000.** Big **mistake!** After grinding and **groaning,** the machine spit out **toilets,** one after **another, endlessly.** Their teeth were **long.** Their eyeballs glowed blood **red.** They looked **fierce, angry,** and **hungry.** Worst of **all,** they talked! The frightened boys fled the **auditorium,** closed the **door,** and ran into Mr. **Krupp.**

Comment: I like the rhetorical fragment, *Big mistake!* Do you think the exclamation point should be there? Or is a period, an understatement, better? I could have created an interesting long sentence with managing semicolons, followed by an exclamatory short sentence: *Their teeth were* **long;** *their eyeballs glowed* **red;** *and they looked fierce, angry and hungry. Worst of all they talked!* The revised long sentence only comprises 15 words and has a nice flow. It shows how you can use a managing semicolon and commas to help the reader. So which is better, the staccato effect of the original short sentences or the smoother rhythm of the revision? You have the tools, make your judgment.

4. Instead of listening to the **children,** Mr. Krupp opened the door to the **auditorium. Another** big **mistake. The** toilets escaped and ran **wild. They** ate **everything! They** consumed **desks, teachers,** and even **children. Everything** and everyone was swallowed **whole. The** school became a great big **mess.** Mr. Krupp began to **whine. After** all the **carnage,** he feared losing his **job.** But George and Harold offered him a **deal,** which he **accepted.** They went back to the PATSY 2000 **and,** after searching through **magazines,** placed a photo of a toilet plunger on **it. After** the machine grated and creaked and **moaned,** the Incredible Roboplunger emerged to do battle with the talking **toilets.**

Comment: In paragraph 4, a rhetorical fragment, *Another big mistake.,* sets up the remainder of the paragraph. Notice the period. I used an exclamation point in the paragraph above and did not want to repeat it here.

The situation described in the story is clearly out of control. For this reason, I placed the point of emphasis after *They ate everything!* Is this one too many or does it work in this context? Also, instead of a period, you might insert a managing semicolon into these two sentences: *Mr. Krupp began to* **whine;** *after all the* **carnage,** *he feared losing his* **job.** This change might reduce the choppiness. Or perhaps that effect is useful.

Finally, only one comma appears in the last sentence. I liked the flow created by omitting pauses. If, however, you want the pauses you have another chance to employ the managing semicolon: *After the machine* **grated, creaked,** *and* **moaned;** *the Incredible Roboplunger emerged to do battle with the talking toilets.* Two semicolons in the same short paragraph, however, are probably one too many. But that's a matter of taste. Tools again.

5. The battle cannot be **described,** but it was **fierce. In** the **end,** the Incredible Roboplunger defeated the talking **toilets,** who coughed up everything they had **eaten. All** emerged **alive, well,** and scratch **free.** George and Harold got their **reward: They** became Principals for the **Day. As** their first **act,** they put Mr. Krupp and the teachers in **detention. Then** they spent the Principal's budget on ice cream and pizza for the **kids.**

Comment: In this fifth paragraph, a connector semicolon could have been placed in the first sentence. But I preferred an introducer comma and the coordinating conjunction, *described, but,*. Also, the forward-looking colon after *reward:* highlights the prize the children received.

Exercise: If you are familiar with the Captain Underpants books, write an essay about one of them. Try to use all the marks you have learned. The actual book that formed the basis of this story is much funnier. If, however, you are not acquainted with these books, your world is a sadder place than it needs to be. In that case, pick a book or story with which you are familiar and write an essay about it. Again, your task is to use all the punctuation tools you have learned.

Some Additional Comments: Each book in the Captain Underpants series begins with Mr. Krupp and the teachers treating the children badly. Nonetheless, Harold and George always change Mr. Krupp into the superhero, Captain Underpants, who saves the world. He is called Captain Underpants because, well, that is his uniform. Mr. Pilkey is not a subtle writer. I did not include the superhero part in this worksheet. You'll have to read it for yourself.

Instead, I emphasized the comedy and punctuation issues. But an ethical point lies underneath the humor. Mr. Krupp placed the children in detention simply because he doesn't like them. What kind of person does that?

Mr. Krupp and the teachers are tyrants, less interested in educating children than controlling them. Although literary types might object to the comparison, Dav Pilkey's and Kurt Vonnegut's works display similarities. Both argue that people, even children, ought to be treated with respect. And both believe that persons in positions of authority should not be cruel or overbearing, especially toward smaller or weaker people.

In the story, Melvin made a mistake when he created the talking toilets. But rather than protecting the children, Mr. Krupp made a bad situation worse. Then he became more worried about himself than the carnage he caused. Aren't these reactions typical of bullies?

Finally, in Dav Pilkey's world, the kids always win over those who would persecute them. I wish this were true more often.

XI.
Improving your Writing Skills and Changing the World

You have now completed ten worksheets. Ten!!! You should feel a sense of accomplishment. Your toolbox of punctuation marks gives you control over sentence and paragraph construction. Its contents mean that in punctuation decisions, as in life, you have choices. In addition, your writing skills have improved with all this practice. And writing well gives you the opportunity to influence others, perhaps to change the world.

You may think changing the world is farfetched. But why not? And why not you? After all, like the superheroes in the Marvel Comics, you now have a superpower. Your abilities, however, are not imaginary; they are practical. You engage readers by informing, entertaining, and persuading them. It's true that most of the time your writing tasks are routine. But your essay persuaded your teacher to purchase a copy of *Captain Underpants.* Your best friend is now learning to draw like Dav Pilkey. And, best of all, fourteen people came to the first meeting of the Captain Underpants fan club! Who knows what will happen as a result? Maybe just a few laughs. Maybe more.

Regardless of the outcome, anything worth doing in life begins with a positive mind set and small steps, such as the ones you have taken here. It's like making your bed each morning. This is a chore, of course. But consider it a practical metaphor: You start the day with a task completed. And if you begin by doing the little tasks well, then the big ones become possible. Moreover, when you've had a miserable day, and you will have many of them, you will come home to a made bed. You will feel better, encouraged to try again tomorrow.[40]

---

[40] These closing paragraphs are indebted to William H. McRaven, *Make Your Bed: Little Things that can Change your life ... and Maybe the World* (New York: Grand Central Publishing, 2017).

Whether you are learning how to use punctuation tools, improve your writing skills, or do anything else, it's hard to accomplish much by youself. Ask for help from friends, teachers, or mentors. Along the way, don't let your will to succeed get in the way of treating others with kindness and respect, regardless of their differences from you. A few of them will become your friends and colleagues. The others will feel better and that, in itself, makes the world a better place.

You probably made mistakes on some of the worksheets. Like everyone, you will fail often in life. Some of these failures will involve more important things than punctuation tools. Absorb the lessons and move on. Never, ever give up! After all, you have learned a great deal and can now turn to other matters.

Your Concluding Ideas Here

_____

_____

_____

_____

_____

_____

_____

_____

_____

_____

# About the Author

I was born in 1946. That date suggests why my young friend Carla calls me, with affection I hope, the Old Man. As a child, I lived in five cities in four widely dispersed states. As a result of these moves, I attended three elementary schools, three middle schools, and two high schools. In 1954, just before a vaccine became available, I contracted polio and spent six weeks in the hospital. I repeated 2nd grade. In elementary school, my mother sent mayonnaise sandwiches in my lunchbox for me to eat. She tried to persuade me that nothing else between the slices was necessary. In high school, I ate large bowls of popcorn as an after-dinner food supplement. On my own at 18, I enrolled in college and stayed there for nine years, eventually earning a Ph.D. from the University of California, Riverside, in 1973.

I succeeded by working hard, very hard. But I also had help and sometimes benefitted from random events. People mentored me, government assistance for the poor became available, and sheer luck stepped in. The lesson I draw from this is that, while everyone works hard, success often depends on assistance and good fortune.

From 1973 to 2008, I taught Sociology at the University of Florida. I also wrote seven books, some of which remain available at Amazon.com. In 2008, my wife and I retired and moved to Durham, NC, home of our three grandchildren. In addition, I play duplicate bridge, enjoy photography, and tutor Hispanic children. I am also active in my church. One thing I have not done is kill an alligator and make a meal of its meat. Maybe someday.

My books:

Leonard Beeghley. *Social Stratification in America: A Critical Analysis of Theory and Research.* Santa Monica, Cal.: Goodyear, 1978.

Jonathan H. Turner, Leonard Beeghley, and Charles Powers. *The Emergence of Sociological Theory.* Homewood, Ill.: Dorsey Press, 1981; 2nd edition 1989 (translated into Chinese), 3rd edition 1995 (translated into Korean), 4th edition 1998, 5th edition 2002, 6th edition 2006, 7th edition 2012 (translated into Portuguese).

Leonard Beeghley. *Living Poorly in America.* New York: Praeger Special Studies, 1983.

Leonard Beeghley. *The Structure of Stratification in the United States.* Boston: Allyn & Bacon, 1989; 2nd edition 1996, 3rd edition 2000, 4th edition 2005, 5th edition 2008.

Leonard Beeghley. *What Does Your Wife Do? Gender and the Transformation of Family Life.* Boulder, CO: Westview Press, 1996.

Leonard Beeghley. *Angles of Vision: How to Understand Social Problems.* Boulder, CO: Westview Press, 1999.

Leonard Beeghley. *Homicide: A Sociological Explanation.* New York: Rowman & Littlefield, 2003.

# Acknowledgments

This workbook began as a series of emails between me and Brenda, the author of the fanboys example. She wanted to improve her punctuation skills and ended up helping start this project.

At that time, Sheridan Baker's book, *The Practical Stylist*, provided my only source on punctuation. Many of the illustrations and explanations from those initial emails reappear here, mainly in the section on commas. In addition, Dr. Baker gave names to each type of comma. It seemed reasonable, then, to also give names to each function of the colon and semicolon as well. This strategy helps organize the material so that it makes sense to readers.

As a native speaker and author, I believed punctuation was easy and, indeed, thought of myself as a pretty good writer. Such hubris. This arrogance was shattered by trying to teach these topics to Hispanic children. They had an annoying habit of asking questions. "That's how you do it in English" is not a good response. Knowing little, I did what college professors do: Research. Many observers teach punctuation. Others teach good writing. A few consider the inherent connection between the two. The footnotes suggest how much I learned from those who know more than I do about these issues.

Some of the Hispanic children I help tutor are mentioned by name in the text. In addition to Brenda, they are Melanie, Carla, Luis, Alan, Liliana, Kevin, Nicolas, Richard, Alexis, and Ronald. My grandchildren, Belle and Abe, also appear. These young people enrich my life in ways that cannot be described. Just so you know, Abe is too young to have hairy knuckles.

It took me several drafts to realize how to make this workbook both interesting and unique compared to others in the field. Dr. Thomas Sinclair and Dr. Mary Anna Hovey took time out of their busy schedules to read and comment on each draft. You may have noticed that I often go for the cheap laugh. They suggested taking out the worst jokes and laugh lines, and I mostly agreed. In addition, by pointing out awkward phrasing and jumbled logic, they helped me sharpen the argument as it developed.

Noahjohn Dittmar and his pupils at Cedar Ridge High School in Hillsborough, NC, field tested the workbook. Mr. Dittmar led the students through the text and they patiently tried the worksheets. In doing so, they identified and saved me from some embarrassing mistakes.

Several people commented on early drafts: Peggy Armstrong, David Balding, Beth Bowling, Dr. Charles Clotfelder, Margaret Dolbow, and Rev. Larry Reimer. When I struggled, they encouraged me. The cover and text of this workbook look attractive because Claudia Fulshaw devoted her time and talent to making it so. She also taught me about how to publish this little tome. Except for the late Sheridan Baker, whom I admire but never met, everyone mentioned here is my friend. Some are young, some are old like me, and some are in between. I am blessed to know each of them.

Any mistakes, omissions, or other problems with the text are my responsibility. But you can help!

Contact Me

Please write to me. Tell me what you think about the book: what you liked and disliked. If you see any mistakes, please tell me about them. I am especially interested in your suggestions about topics for new worksheets.

My email address is: leonardbeeghley@gmail.com.

Thank you.